An Outback Marriage
A Story of Australian Life

by

A. B. Paterson

An Outback Marriage
A Story of Australian Life
by A. B. Paterson

Copyright © 2024

All Rights reserved.

No part of this publication may be reproduced, stored in a retrieval system, or transmitted in any form or by any means, electronic, mechanical, photocopying or Otherwise, without the written permission of the publisher.
The author/editor asserts the moral right to be identified as the author/editor of this work.

ISBN: 978-93-64280-56-3

Published by

DOUBLE 9 BOOKS
2/13-B, Ansari Road
Daryaganj, New Delhi – 110002
info@double9books.com
www.double9books.com
Tel. 011-40042856

This book is under public domain

ABOUT THE AUTHOR

Andrew Barton Banjo Paterson (1864–1941) was a renowned Australian poet, journalist, and author, celebrated for his vibrant depictions of rural and outback life. Born in Narrambla near Orange, New South Wales, Paterson was raised in the country, which deeply influenced his writing and worldview. Paterson's literary career took off with the publication of his first poems in *The Bulletin*, a popular Australian magazine. He adopted the pen name The Banjo after a favorite horse, and it quickly became synonymous with his work. Paterson is best known for his poetry and ballads that celebrate the Australian bush and its people. His most famous works include: **The Man from Snowy River (1890):** A narrative poem that became an iconic representation of the Australian outback spirit. **Waltzing Matilda (1895):** Often referred to as Australia's unofficial national anthem, this song tells the story of a swagman (itinerant worker) and has become deeply ingrained in Australian culture. In his later years, Paterson continued to write and publish, contributing to the rich tapestry of Australian literature. He died in Sydney in 1941, leaving behind a legacy that continues to influence Australian culture and identity.

Paterson's work is celebrated for its authentic portrayal of the Australian landscape and the spirit of its people. His ability to capture the essence of the bush and its characters has made him a beloved figure in Australian literature, and his poems and stories remain timeless classics.

CONTENTS

CHAPTER I
IN THE CLUB 7

CHAPTER II
A DINNER FOR FIVE 13

CHAPTER III
IN PUSH SOCIETY 17

CHAPTER IV
THE OLD STATION 24

CHAPTER V
THE COMING OF THE HEIRESS 30

CHAPTER VI
A COACH ACCIDENT 38

CHAPTER VII
MR. BLAKE'S RELATIONS 46

CHAPTER VIII
AT THE HOMESTEAD 49

CHAPTER IX
SOME VISITORS 54

CHAPTER X
A LAWYER IN THE BUSH 59

CHAPTER XI
A WALK IN THE MOONLIGHT 63

CHAPTER XII
MR. BLAKE BREAKS HIS ENGAGEMENT 69

CHAPTER XIII
THE RIVALS 72

CHAPTER XIV
RED MICK AND HIS SHEEP DOGS 76

CHAPTER XV
A PROPOSAL AND ITS RESULTS 85

CHAPTER XVI
THE ROAD TO NO MAN'S LAND 90

CHAPTER XVII
CONSIDINE 99

CHAPTER XVIII
THE WILD CATTLE 104

CHAPTER XIX
A CHANCE ENCOUNTER 111

CHAPTER XX
A CONSULTATION AT KILEY'S 119

CHAPTER XXI
NO COMPROMISE 125

CHAPTER XXII
A NURSE AND HER ASSISTANT 131

CHAPTER XXIII
HUGH GOES IN SEARCH 135

CHAPTER XXIV
THE SECOND SEARCH FOR CONSIDINE 139

CHAPTER XXV
IN THE BUFFALO CAMP 146

CHAPTER XXVI
THE SAVING OF CONSIDINE 150

CHAPTER XXVII
THE REAL CERTIFICATE 159

CHAPTER XXVIII
A LEGAL BATTLE 162

CHAPTER XXIX
RACES AND A WIN 167

CHAPTER I
IN THE CLUB

It was a summer's evening in Sydney, and the north-east wind that comes down from New Guinea and the tropical islands over leagues of warm sea, brought on its wings a heavy depressing moisture. In the streets people walked listlessly, perspired, mopped themselves, and abused their much-vaunted climate. Everyone who could manage it was out of town, either on the heights of Moss Vale or the Blue Mountains, escaping from the Inferno of Sydney.

In the Cassowary Club, weary, pallid waiters brought iced drinks to such of the members as were condemned to spend the summer in town. The gong had sounded, and in ones and twos members shuffled out of the smoking-room, and went in to dinner. At last only three were left talking at the far end of the big, empty smoking-room, like three small stage conspirators at the end of a very large robbers' cavern.

One was a short, fat, red-faced man, who looked like a combination of sea-captain and merchant, and who was the local representative of a big English steamship company. His connection with the mercantile marine had earned him his nickname of "The Bo'sun." By his side sat Pinnock, a lean and bilious-looking solicitor; the third man was an English globe-trotter, a colourless sort of person, of whom no one took any particular notice until they learnt that he was the eldest son of a big Scotch whisky manufacturer, and had £10,000 a year of his own. Then they suddenly discovered that he was a much smarter fellow than he looked. The three were evidently waiting for somebody. The "Bo'sun" had a grievance, and was relieving his mind by speech. He walked up and down between the smoking-room chairs, brandishing a telegram as he talked, while the attorney and the globe-trotter lay back on the lounge and admired his energy.

"I call it a shame," he said, facing round on them suddenly; "I could have got up to Moss Vale for a day or two, and now old Grant of Kuryong wires me to meet and entertain a new chum. Just listen to this: 'Young Carew, friend of mine, on *Carthaginia*. Will you meet him and show him round; oblige me — W. G. Grant.' I met the old fellow once or twice at dinner, when he was in town for the sheep sales, and on the strength of that he foists an unknown callow new chum on to me. People are always doing that kind of thing."

"Leave his friend alone, then," said Pinnock; "don't have anything to do with him. I know his sort—Government House young man the first week, Coffee Palace at two shillings a night the second week, boiler on the wharf the third week, Central Police Court the fourth week, and then exit so far as all decent people are concerned."

The Bo'sun stuffed the telegram into his pocket and sat down.

"Oh, I don't suppose he'll be so bad," he said. "I've asked him here to-night to see what he's like, and if he's no good I'll drop him. It's the principle I object to. Country people are always at this sort of thing. They'd ask me to meet an Alderney bull and entertain him till they send for him. What am I to do with an unknown new chum? I'd sooner have an Alderney bull—he'd be easier to arrange for. He'd stop where he was put, anyhow."

Here Gillespie, the globe-trotter, cut into the conversation. "I knew a Jim Carew in England," he said, "and if this is the same man you will have no trouble taking care of him. He was a great man at his 'Varsity—triple blue, or something of the sort. He can row and run and fight and play football, and all that kind of thing. Very quiet-spoken sort of chap—rather pretends to be a simple sort of Johnny, don't you know, but he's a regular demon, I believe. Got into a row at a music-hall one night, and threw the chucker-out in among a lot of valuable pot plants, and irretrievably ruined him."

"Nice sort of man," said the Bo'sun. "I've seen plenty of his sort, worse luck; he'll be borrowing fivers after the first week. I'll put him on to you fellows."

The globe-trotter smiled a sickly smile, and changed the subject. "What's old Grant like—the man he's going to? Squatter man, I suppose?"

"Oh, yes, and one of the real old sort, too," interposed Pinnock, "perfect gentleman, you know, but apt to make himself deuced unpleasant if everything doesn't go exactly to suit him; sort of chap who thinks that everyone who doesn't agree with him ought to be put to death at once. He had a row with his shearers one year, and offered Jack Delaney a new Purdey gun if he'd fire the first two charges into the shearers' camp at night."

"Ha!" said Gillespie. "That's his sort, eh? Well, if this Carew is the Carew I mean, he and the old fellow will be well met. They'll about do for each other in the first week or two."

"No great loss, either," said the Bo'sun. "Anyhow I've asked this new chum to dinner to-night, and Charlie Gordon's coming too. He was in my office to-day, but hadn't heard of the new chum. Gordon's a member now."

"What's he like?" said Gillespie. "Anything like the gentleman that wanted the shearers killed?"

"Oh, no; a good fellow," said the Bo'sun, taking a sip of sherry. "He manages stations for Grant, and the old man has kept him out on the back-stations nearly all his life. He was out in the Gulf-country in the early days—got starved out in droughts, swept away in floods, lost in the bush, speared by blacks, and all that sort of thing, in the days when men camped under bushes and didn't wear shirts. Gone a bit queer in the head, I think, but a good chap for all that."

"How did this Grant make all his money" asked Gillespie. "He's awfully well off, isn't he? Stations everywhere? Is he any relation to Gordon?"

"No; old Gordon—Charlie's father—used to have the money. He had a lot of stations in the old days, and employed Grant as a manager. Grant was a new chum Scotchman with no money, but a demon for hard work, and the most headstrong, bad-tempered man that ever lived—hard to hold at any time. After he'd worked for Gordon for awhile he went to the diggings and made a huge pile; and when old Gordon got a bit short of cash he took Grant into partnership."

"It must have been funny for a man to have his old manager as a partner!"

"It wasn't at all funny for Gordon," said the lawyer, grimly. "Anything but funny. They each had stations of their own outside the partnership, and all Gordon's stations went wrong, and Grant's went right. It never seemed to rain on Gordon's stations, while Grant's had floods. So Gordon got short of money again and borrowed from Grant, and when he was really in a fix Grant closed on him and sold him out for good and all."

"What an old screw! What did he do that for?"

"Just pure obstinacy—Gordon had contradicted him or something, so he sold him up just to show which was right."

"And what did Gordon do after he was sold up?"

"Died, and didn't leave a penny. So then Bully Grant wheeled round and gave Gordon's widow a station to live on, and fixed the two sons up managing his stations. Goodness knows how much he's worth now. Doesn't even know it himself."

"And has he no children? Was he ever married?"

The lawyer lit a cigarette and puffed at it.

"He went to England and got married; there's a daughter. The wife's dead; the daughter is in England still—never been out here. There's a story that before he made his money he married a bush girl up on the station, but no one believes that. The daughter in England will get everything when he dies. A chance for you, Gillespie. Go home and marry her—she'll be worth nearly a million of money."

"I'll think about it," said the globe-trotter.

As he spoke a buttony boy came up to the Bo'sun.

"Gentleman to see you, sir," he said. "Mr. Carew, sir."

The Bo'sun hurried off to bring in his guest, while Pinnock called after him—"Mind your eye, Bo'sun. Be civil to him. See that he doesn't kill a waiter or two on the way up. Not but what he'd be welcome to do it, for all the good they are here," he added, gloomily, taking another sip of his sherry and bitters; and before he had finished it the Bo'sun and his guest entered the room.

They had expected to see a Hercules, a fiery-faced, fierce-eyed man. This was merely a broad-shouldered, well-built, well-groomed youth, about twenty-three years of age; his face was square and rather stolid, clean-shaven, brown-complexioned, with honest eyes and a firm-set mouth. As he stood at the door he adopted the wooden expression that a University man always wears in the presence of strangers. He said nothing on being introduced to Pinnock; and when the globe-trotter came up and claimed acquaintance, defining himself as "Gillespie of Balliol," the stranger said he didn't remember him, and regarded him with an aspect of armed neutrality. After a sherry and bitters he thawed a little, and the Bo'sun started to cross-examine him.

"Mr. Grant of Kuryong wired to me about you," he said. "I suppose you came in the *Carthaginia*?"

"Yes," said the stranger, speaking in the regulation English University voice, a little deeper than usual. "I left her at Adelaide. I'm out for some bush experience, don't you know. I'll get you to tell me some place to stop at till I leave, if you don't mind."

His manner was distinctly apologetic, and he seemed anxious to give as little trouble as possible.

"Oh! you stop here," said the Bo'sun. "I'll have you made an honorary member. They'll do you all right here."

"That's awfully good of you. Thanks very much indeed."

"Oh! not at all. You'll find the club not so bad, and a lot better than where you're going with old Grant. He's a regular demon to make fellows work. It's pretty rough on the stations sometimes."

"Ah! yes; awf'lly rough, I believe. Quite frightened me, what I heard of it, don't you know. Still, I suppose one must expect to rough it a bit. Eh, what!"

"Charlie Gordon will he here in a minute," said the Bo'sun. "He can tell you all about it. Here he is now," he added, as the door swung open and the long-waited-for guest entered the room.

The newcomer was unmistakably a man from Far Out; tall, wiry-framed, and very dark, and so spare and lean of figure that he did not seem to have an ounce of superfluous flesh anywhere. His face was as hard and impassive as a Red Indian's, and looked almost black by contrast with his white shirt-front. So did his hands. He had thin straight hair, high cheek-bones, and a drooping black moustache. But the eyes were the most remarkable feature. Very keen and piercing they were, deep-set in the head; even when he was looking straight at anyone he seemed to be peering into endless space through the man in front of him. Such eyes men get from many years of staring over great stretches of sunlit plain where no colour relieves the blinding glare—nothing but dull grey clumps of saltbush and the dull green Mitchell grass.

His whole bearing spoke of infinite determination and self-reliance—the square chin, the steadfast eyes, telling their tale as plainly as print. In India he might have passed for an officer of native cavalry in mufti; but when he spoke he used the curious nasal drawl of the far-out bushman, the slow deliberate speech that comes to men who are used to passing months with the same companions in the unhurried Australian bush. Occasionally he lapsed into reveries, out of which he would come with a start and break in on other people's conversation, talking them down with a serene indifference to their feelings.

"Come out to old man Grant, have you?" he drawled to Carew, when the ceremonies of introduction were over. "Well, I can do something better for you than that. I want a mate for my next trip, and a rough lonely hot trip it'll be. But don't you make any mistake. The roughest and hottest I can show you will be child's play to having anything to do with Grant. You come with me."

"Hadn't I better see Mr. Grant first?"

"No, he won't care. The old man doesn't take much notice of new chums—he gets them out by the bushel. He might meet a man at dinner in

England and the man might say, "Grant, you've got some stations. I've got a young fellow that's no use at home—or anywhere else for that matter—can't you oblige me, and take him and keep him out of mischief for a while?" And if the old man had had about a bottle of champagne, he'd say, "Yes, I'll take him—for a premium," or if he'd had two bottles, he'd say, "Send along your new chum—I'll make a man of him or break his neck." And perhaps in the next steamer out the fellow comes, and Grant just passes him on to me. Never looks at him, as likely as not. Don't you bother your head about Grant—you come with me."

As he drawled out his last sentence, a move was made to dinner; so the Englishman was spared the pain of making any comments on his own unimportance in Mr. Grant's eyes, and they trooped into the dining-room in silence.

CHAPTER II
A DINNER FOR FIVE

A club dining-room in Australia is much like one in any other part of the world. Even at the Antipodes—though the seasons are reversed, and the foxes have wings—we still shun the club bore, and let him have a table to himself; the head waiter usually looks a more important personage than any of the members or guests; and men may be seen giving each other dinners from much the same ignoble motives as those which actuate their fellows elsewhere. In the Cassowary Club, on the night of which we tell, the Bo'sun was giving his dinner of necessity to honour the draft of hospitality drawn on him by Grant. At the next table a young solicitor was entertaining his one wealthy client; near by a band of haggard University professors were dining a wandering scientist, all hair and spectacles—both guest and hosts drinking mineral waters and such horrors; while beyond them a lot of racing men were swilling champagne and eating and talking as heartily as so many navvies. A few squatters, down from their stations, had fore-gathered at the centre table, where each was trying to make out that he had had less rain than the others. The Bo'sun and his guests were taken in hand by the head waiter, who formerly had been at a London Club, and was laying himself out to do his best; he had seen that Gillespie had "Wanderers' Club" on his cards, and he knew, and thanked his stars that he did know, what "Wanderers' Club" on a man's card meant. His fellow-waiters, to whom he usually referred as "a lot of savages," were unfortunately in ignorance of the social distinction implied by membership of such a club.

For a time there was nothing but the usual commonplace talk, while the soup and fish were disposed of; when they reached the champagne and the entrées, things become more homelike and conversation flowed. A bushman, especially when primed with champagne, is always ready to give his tongue a run—and when he has two open-mouthed new chums for audience, as Gordon had, the only difficulty is to stop him before bed-time; for long silent rides on the plain, and lonely camps at night, give him a lot of enforced silence that he has to make up for later.

"Where are you from last, Gordon?" said the Bo'sun. "Haven't seen you in town for a long time."

"I've been hunting wild geese," drawled the man from far back, screwing up one eye and inspecting a glass of champagne, which he drank off at a gulp. "That's what I do most of my time now. The old man—Grant, you know—my boss—he's always hearing of mobs of cattle for sale, and if I'm down in the south-west the mob is sure to be up in the far north-east, but it's all one to him. He wires to me to go and inspect them quick and lively before someone else gets them, and I ride and drive and coach hundreds of miles to get at some flat-sided pike-horned mob of brutes without enough fat on them to oil a man's hair with. I've to go right away out back now and take over a place that the old man advanced some money on. He was fool enough, or someone was fool enough for him, to advance five thousand pounds on a block of new country with five thousand cattle on it—book-muster, you know, and half the cattle haven't been seen for years, and the other half are dead, I expect. Anyhow, the man that borrowed the money is ruined, and I have to go up and take over the station."

"What do you call a book-muster?" said the globe-trotter, who was spending a month in the country, and would naturally write a book on it.

"Book-muster, book-muster? Why, a book-muster is something like dead-reckoning on a ship. You know what dead-reckoning is, don't you? If a captain can't see the sun he allows for how fast the ship is going, and for the time run and the currents, and all that, and then reckons up where he is. I travelled with a captain once, and so long as he stuck to dead-reckoning he was all right. He made out we were off Cairns, and that's just where we were; because we struck the Great Barrier Reef, and became a total wreck ten minutes after. With the cattle it's just the same. You'll reckon the cattle that you started with, add on each year's calves, subtract all that you sell,—that is, if you ever do sell any—and allow for deaths, and what the blacks spear and the thieves steal. Then you work out the total, and you say, 'There ought to be five thousand cattle on the place,' but you never get 'em. I've got to go and find five thousand cattle in the worst bit of brigalow scrub in the north."

"Where do you say this place is?" said Pinnock. "It's called No Man's Land, and it's away out back near where the buffalo-shooters are. It'll take about a month to get there. The old man's in a rare state of mind at being let in. He's up at Kuryong now, driving my brother Hugh out of his mind. Hugh would as soon have an attack of faceache as see old Bully looming up the track. Every time he goes up he shifts every blessed sheep out of every paddock, and knocks seven years' growth out of them putting them through the yards; then he overhauls the store, and if there's a box of matches short he'll keep Hugh up half the night to account for it. He sacks all the good men and raises the wages of the loafers, and then comes back to Sydney quite pleased; it's a little holiday to him. You come along with me, Carew, and let old Bully alone. What did you come out for? Colonial experience?"

An Englishman hates talking about himself, and Carew rather hesitated. Then he came out with it awkwardly, like a man repeating a lesson.

"Did you ever meet a man named Considine out here?" he said.

"Lots of them," said Gordon promptly—"lots of them. Why, I had a man named Considine working for me, and he thought he got bitten by a snake, so his mates ran him twenty miles into Bourke between two horses to keep him from going to sleep, giving him a nip of whisky every twenty minutes; and when he got to Bourke he wasn't bitten at all, but he died of alcoholic poisoning. What about this Considine, anyhow? What do you want him for?"

The Englishman felt like dropping the subject altogether, not feeling quite sure that he was not being laughed at. However, he decided to go through with it.

"It's rather a long story, but it boils down to this," he said. "I'm looking for a Patrick Henry Considine, but I don't know what he's like. I don't know whether there is such a chap, in fact, but if there is, I've got to find him. A great-uncle of mine died out here a long while ago, and we believe he left a son; and if there is such a son, it turns out that he would be entitled to a heap of money. It has been heaping up for years in Chancery, and all that sort of thing, you know," he added, vaguely. "My people thought I might meet him out here, don't you know—and he could go home and get all the cash, you see. They've been advertising for him."

"And what good will it do you," drawled Gordon, "supposing you do find him? Where do you come in?"

"Oh, it doesn't do me much good, except that if there is such a Johnny, and he dies without making a will, then the money would all come to my people. But if there isn't, it all goes to another branch of the family."

Gordon thought the matter over for a while. "What you want," he said, "is to find this man, and to find him dead. If we come across him away in the back country, we'll soon arrange his death for you, if you make it worth while. Nasty gun accident, or something like that, you know."

"I wouldn't like anyone to shoot him," said the Englishman.

"Well, you come with me, and we'll find him," said Gordon.

By this time dinner was over. The waiters began to turn out the lights on the vacant tables; and, as the party rose it was arranged *nem. con.*, and with much enthusiasm, that Carew should accompany Gordon on his trip to No Man's Land, and that Gordon should, by all means in his power, aid and abet Carew in his search for Considine.

Then, all talking together, and somewhat loudly, they strutted into the smoking-room.

CHAPTER III
IN PUSH SOCIETY

The passing of the evening afterwards is the only true test of a dinner's success. Many a good dinner, enlivened with wine and made brilliant with repartee, has died out in gloom. The guests have all said their best things during the meal, and nothing is left but to smoke moodily and look at the clock. Our heroes were not of that mettle. They meant to have some sort of fun, and the various amusements of Sydney were canvassed. It was unanimously voted too hot for the theatres, ditto for billiards. There were no supporters for a proposal to stop in the smoking-room and drink, and gambling in the card-rooms had no attractions on such a night. At last Gordon hit off a scent. "What do you say," he drawled, "if we go and have a look at a dancing saloon—one of these larrikin dancing saloons?"

"I'd like it awfully," said one Englishman.

"Most interesting" said the other. "I've heard such a lot about the Australian larrikin. What they call a basher in England, isn't it? eh, what? Sort of rough that lays for you with a pal and robs you, eh?"

The Bo'sun rang for cigars and liqueurs, and then answered the question. "Pretty much the same as a basher," he said, "but with a lot more science and dog-cunning about him. They go in gangs, and if you hit one of the gang, all the rest will 'deal with you,' as they call it. If they have to wait a year to get you, they'll wait, and get you alone some night or other and set on to you. They jump on a man if they get him down, too. Oh, they're regular beauties."

"Rather roughish sort of Johnnies, eh?" said the Englishman. "But we might go and see the dancing—no harm in that."

Pinnock said he had to go back to his office; the globe-trotter didn't care about going out at night; and the Bo'sun tried to laugh the thing off. "You don't catch me going," he said. "There's nothing to be seen—just a lot of flash young rowdies dancing. You'll gape at them, and they'll gape at you, and you'll feel rather a pair of fools, and you'll come away. Better stop and have a rubber."

"If you dance with any of their women, you get her particular fancy-man on to you, don't you?" asked Gordon. "It's years since I was at that sort of place myself."

The Bo'sun, who knew nothing about it, assumed the Sir Oracle at once.

"I don't suppose their women would dance with you if you paid 'em five shillings a step," he said. "There'd certainly be a fight if they did. Are you fond of fighting, Carew?"

"Not a bit," replied that worthy. "Never fight if you can help it. No chap with any sense ever does."

"That's like me," said Gordon. "I'd sooner run a mile than fight, any time. I'm like a rat if I'm cornered, but it takes a man with a stockwhip to corner me. I never start fighting till I'm done running. But we needn't get into a row. I vote we go. Will you come, Carew?"

"Oh, yes; I'd like to," said the Englishman. "I don't suppose we need get into a fight."

So, after many jeers from the Bo'sun, and promises to come back and tell him all about it, Carew and Gordon sallied forth, a pair of men as capable of looking after themselves as one would meet in a day's march. Stepping into the street they called a cab.

"Where to, sir?" asked the cabman.

"Nearest dancing saloon," said Gordon, briefly.

"Nearest darncin' saloon," said the cabman. "There ain't no parties to-night, sir; it's too 'ot."

"We're not expecting to drop into a ballroom without being asked, thank you," said Gordon. "We want to go to one of those saloons where you pay a shilling to go in. Some place where the larrikins go."

"Ho! is that it, sir?" said the cabman, with a grin. "Well, I'll take you to a noo place, most selectest place I know. Git up, 'orse." And off they rattled through the quiet streets, turning corners and crossing tramlines every fifty yards apparently, and bumping against each other in the most fraternal manner.

Soon the cab pulled up in a narrow, ill-lit street, at the open door of a dingy house. Instructing the cabman to wait, they hustled upstairs, to be confronted at the top by a man who took a shilling from each, and then was not sure whether he would admit them. He didn't seem to like their form exactly, and muttered something to a by-stander as they went in. They saw a long, low room, brilliantly lighted by flaring gas jets. Down one side, on wooden forms, was seated a row of flashily-dressed girls—larrikin-esses on their native heath, barmaids from cheap, disreputable hotels, shop girls, factory girls—all sharp-faced and pert, young in years, but old in knowledge of evil. The demon of mischief peeped out of their quick-moving, restless eyes. They had elaborate fringes, and their short dresses exhibited well-turned ankles and legs.

A large notice on the wall stated that "Gentlemen must not dance with nails in their boots. Gentlemen must not dance together."

"That blocks us," said Gordon, pointing to the notice. "Can't dance together, no matter how much we want to. Look at these fellows here."

Opposite the women sat or lounged a score or two of youths—wiry, hard-faced little fellows, for the most part, with scarcely a sizeable man amongst them. They were all clothed in "push" evening dress—black bell-bottomed pants, no waistcoat, very short black paget coat, white shirt with no collar, and a gaudy neckerchief round the bare throat. Their boots were marvels, very high in the heel and picked out with all sorts of colours down the sides. They looked "varminty" enough for anything; but the shifty eyes, low foreheads, and evil faces gave our two heroes a sense of disgust. The Englishman thought that all the stories he had heard of the Australian larrikin must be exaggerated, and that any man who was at all athletic could easily hold his own among such a poor-looking lot. The whole spectacle was disappointing. The most elaborately decorous order prevailed; no excitement or rough play was noticeable, and their expedition seemed likely to be a failure.

The bushman stared down the room with far-seeing eyes, apparently looking at nothing, and contemplated the whole show with bored indifference.

"Nothing very dazzling about this," he said. "I'm afraid we can't show you anything very exciting here. Better go back to the club, eh?"

Just then the band (piano and violin) struck up a slow, laboured waltz, "Bid me Good-bye and go," and each black-coated male, with languid self-possession, strolled across the room, seized a lady by the arm, jerked her to her feet without saying a syllable, and commenced to dance in slow, convulsive movements, making a great many revolutions for very little progress. Two or three girls were left sitting, as their partners were talking in a little knot at the far end of the room; one among them was conspicuously pretty, and she began to ogle Carew in a very pronounced way.

"There's one hasn't got a partner," said Gordon. "Good-looking Tottie, too. Go and ask her to dance. See what she says."

The Englishman hesitated for a second. "I don't like asking a perfect stranger to dance," he said.

"Go on," said Gordon, "it's all right. She'll like it."

Carew drew down his cuffs, squared his shoulders, assumed his most absolutely stolid drawing-room manner, and walked across the room, a gleaming vision of splendour in his immaculate evening dress.

"May I—er—have the pleasure of this dance?" he said, with elaborate politeness.

The girl giggled a little, but said nothing, then rose and took his arm.

As she did so, a youth among the talkers at the other end of the room looked round, and stared for a second. Then he moistened his fingers with his tongue, smoothed the hair on his temples, and with elbows held out from his sides, shoulders hunched up, and under-jaw stuck well out, bore down on Carew and the girl, who were getting under way when he came up. Taking not the slightest notice of Carew, he touched the girl on the shoulder with a sharp peremptory tap, and brought their dance to a stop.

"'Ere," he said, in commanding tones. "'Oo are you darncin' with?"

"I'm darncin' with 'im," answered the girl, pertly, indicating the Englishman with a jerk of her head.

"Ho, you're darncin' with 'im, are you? 'E brought you 'ere, p'r'aps?"

"No, he didn't," she said.

"No," said he. "You know well enough 'e didn't."

While this conversation was going on, the English-man maintained an attitude of dignified reserve, leaving it to the lady to decide who was to be the favoured man. At last he felt it was hardly right for an Oxford man, and a triple blue at that, to be discussed in this contemptuous way by a larrikin and his "donah," so he broke into the discussion, perhaps a little abruptly, but using his most polished style.

"I—ah—asked this lady to dance, and if she—er—will do me the honour," he said, "I—"

"Oh! you arst 'er to darnce? And what right 'ad you to arst 'er to darnce, you lop-eared rabbit?" interrupted the larrikin, raising his voice as he warmed to his subject. "I brought 'er 'ere. I paid the shillin'. Now then, you take your 'ook," he went on, pointing sternly to the door, and talking as he would to a disobedient dog. "Go on, now. Take your 'ook."

The Englishman said nothing, but his jaw set ominously. The girl giggled, delighted at being the centre of so much observation. The band stopped playing, and the dancers crowded round. Word was passed down that it was a "toff darncin' with Nugget's donah," and from various parts of the room black-coated duplicates of Nugget hurried swiftly to the scene.

The doorkeeper turned to Gordon. "You'd best get your mate out o' this," he said. "These are the Rocks Push, and they'll deal with him all right."

"Deal with him, will they?" said Gordon, looking at the gesticulating Nugget. "They'll bite off more than they can chew if they interfere with him. This is just his form, a row like this. He's a bit of a champion in a rough-and-tumble, I believe."

"Is he?" said the doorkeeper, sardonically. "Well, look 'ere, now, you take it from me, if there's a row Nugget will spread him out as flat as a newspaper. They've all been in the ring in their time, these coves. There's Nugget, and Ginger, and Brummy—all red 'ot. You get him away!"

Meanwhile the Englishman's ire was gradually rising. He was past the stage of considering whether it was worth while to have a fight over a factory girl in a shilling dancing saloon, and the desire for battle blazed up in his eyes. He turned and confronted Nugget.

"You go about your business," he said, dropping all the laboured politeness out of his tones. "If she likes to dance—"

He got no further. A shrill whistle rang through the room; a voice shouted, "Don't 'it 'im; 'ook 'im!" His arms were seized from behind and pinioned to his sides. The lights were turned out. Somebody in front hit him a terrific crack in the eye at the same moment that someone else administered a violent kick from the rear. He was propelled by an invisible force to the head of the stairs, and then—whizz! down he went in one prodigious leap, clear from the top to the first landing.

Here, in pitch-darkness, he grappled one of his assailants. For a few seconds they swayed and struggled, and then rolled down the rest of the stairs, over and over each other, grappling and clawing, each trying to tear the other's shirt off. When they rolled into the street, Carew discovered that he had hold of Charlie Gordon.

They sat up and looked at each other. Then they made a simultaneous rush for the stairs, but the street door was slammed in their faces. They kicked it violently, but without result, except that a mob of faces looked out of the first-floor window and hooted, and a bucket of water was emptied over them. A crowd collected as if by magic, and the spectacle of two gentlemen in evening dress trying to kick in the door of a shilling dancing saloon afforded it unmitigated delight.

"'Ere's two toffs got done in all right," said one.

"What O! Won't she darnce with you?" said another; and somebody from the back threw banana peel at them.

Charlie recovered his wits first. The Englishman was fairly berserk with rage, and glared round on the bystanders as if he contemplated a rush among them. The cabman put an end to the performance. He was tranquil and unemotional, and he soothed them down and coaxed them into the cab. The band in the room above resumed the dreamy waltz music of "Bid me Good-bye and go!" and they went.

Carew subsided into the corner, breathing hard and feeling his eye. Charlie leant forward and peered out into the darkness. They were nearly at the club before they spoke. Then he said, "Well, I'm blessed! We made a nice mess of that, didn't we?"

"I'd like to have got one fair crack at some of 'em," said the Englishman, with heartfelt earnestness. "Couldn't we go back now?"

"No what's the good? We'd never get in. Let the thing alone. We needn't say anything about it. If once it gets known that we were chucked out, we'll never hear the last of it. Are you marked at all?"

"Got an awful swipe in the eye," replied the other briefly.

"I've got a cut lip, and my head nearly screwed off. You did that. I'll know the place again. Some day we'll get a few of the right sort to come with us, and we'll just go there quietly, as if we didn't mean anything, and then, all of a sudden, we'll turn in and break the whole place up! Come and have a drink now."

They had a silent drink in the deserted club. The mind of each was filled with a sickening sense of defeat, and without much conversation they retired to bed. They thanked heaven that the Bo'sun, Pinnock, and Gillespie had disappeared.

Even then Fate hadn't quite finished with the bushman. A newly-joined member of the club, he had lived a life in which he had to shift for himself, and the ways of luxury were new to him. Consequently, when he awoke next morning and saw a man moving with cat-like tread about his room, absolutely taking the money out of his clothes before his very eyes, he sprang out of bed with a bound and half-throttled the robber. Then, of course, it turned out that it was only the bedroom waiter, who was taking his clothes away to brush them. This *contretemps*, on top of the overnight mishap, made him determined to get away from town with all speed. When he looked in the glass, he found his lip so much swelled that his moustache stuck out in front like the bowsprit of a ship. At breakfast he joined the Englishman, who had an eye with as many colours as an opal, not to mention a tired look and dusty boots.

"Are you only just up?" asked Charlie, as they contemplated each other.

Carew had resumed his mantle of stolidity, but he coloured a little at the question. "I've been out for a bit of a walk round town," he said. "Fact is," he added in a sudden burst of confidence, "I've been all over town lookin' for that place where we were last night. Couldn't find anything like it at all."

Charlie laughed at his earnestness. "Oh, bother the place," he said. "If you had found it, there wouldn't have been any of them there. Now, about ourselves—we can't show out like this. We'd better be off to-day, and no one need know anything about it. Besides, I half-killed a waiter this morning. I thought he was some chap stealing my money, when he only wanted to take my clothes away to brush 'em. Sooner we're out of town the better. I'll wire to the old man that I've taken you with me."

So saying, they settled down to breakfast, and by tacit agreement avoided the club for the rest of the day.

Before leaving, Charlie had to call and interview Pinnock, and left Carew waiting outside while he went in. He didn't want to parade their injuries, and knew that Carew's eye would excite remark; but by keeping his upper lip well drawn over his teeth, he hoped his own trouble would escape notice.

"Seems a harmless sort of chap, that new chum," said Pinnock.

"He'll do all right," said Charlie casually. "I've met his sort before. He's not such a fool as he lets on to be. Shouldn't wonder if he killed somebody before he gets back here, anyhow."

"How did you get on at the dancing saloon?" asked Pinnock.

"Oh, slow enough. Nothing worth seeing. Good-bye."

They sneaked on board the steamer without meeting the Bo'sun or anybody, and before evening were well on their way to No Man's Land.

CHAPTER IV
THE OLD STATION

There are few countries in the world with such varieties of climate as Australia, and though some stations are out in the great, red-hot, frying wastes of the Never-Never, others are up in the hills where a hot night is a thing unknown, where snow falls occasionally, and where it is no uncommon thing to spend a summer's evening by the side of a roaring fire. In the matter of improvements, too, stations vary greatly. Some are in a wilderness, with fittings to match; others have telephones between homestead and out-stations, the jackeroos dress for dinner, and the station hands are cowed into touching their hats and saying "Sir." Also stations are of all sizes, and the man who is considered quite a big squatter in the settled districts is thought small potatoes by the magnate "out back," who shears a hundred and fifty thousand sheep, and has an overdraft like the National Debt.

Kuryong was a hill-country station of about sixty thousand acres all told; but they were good acres, as no one knew better than old Bully Grant, the owner, of whose history and disposition we heard something from Pinnock at the club. It was a highly improved place, with a fine homestead—thanks to Bully Grant's money, for in the old days it had been a very different sort of place—and its history is typical of the history of hundreds of others.

When Andrew Gordon first bought it, it was held under lease from the Crown, and there were no improvements to speak of. The station homestead, so lovingly descanted upon in the advertisement, consisted of a two-roomed slab hut; the woolshed, where the sheep were shorn, was made of gumtree trunks roofed with bark. The wool went down to Sydney, and station supplies came back, in huge waggons drawn by eighteen or twenty bullocks, that travelled nine miles a day on a journey of three hundred miles. There were no neighbours except at the township of Kiley's Crossing, which consisted of two public-houses and a store. It was a rough life for the young squatter, and evidently he found it lonely; for on a visit to Sydney he fell in love with and married a dainty girl of French descent. Refined, well-educated, and fragile-looking, she seemed about the last person in the world to take out to a slab-hut homestead as a squatter's wife.

But there is an old saying that blood will tell; and with all the courage of her Huguenot ancestry she faced the roughness and discomforts of bush life. On her arrival at the station the old two-roomed hut was plastered and whitewashed, additional rooms were built, and quite a neat little home was the result. Seasons were good, and the young squatter might have gone on shearing sheep and selling fat stock till the end of his life but for the advent of free selection in 1861.

In that year the Legislature threw open all leasehold lands to the public for purchase on easy terms and conditions. The idea was to settle an industrious peasantry on lands hitherto leased in large blocks to the squatters. This brought down a flood of settlement on Kuryong. At the top end of the station there was a chain of mountains, and the country was rugged and patchy—rich valleys alternating with ragged hills. Here and there about the run were little patches of specially good land, which were soon snapped up. The pioneers of these small settlers were old Morgan Donohoe and his wife, who had built the hotel at Kiley's Crossing; and, on their reports, all their friends and relatives, as they came out of the "ould country," worked their way to Kuryong, and built little bits of slab and bark homesteads in among the mountains. The rougher the country, the better they liked it. They were a horse-thieving, sheep-stealing breed, and the talents which had made them poachers in the old country soon made them champion bushmen in their new surroundings. The leader of these mountain settlers was one Doyle, a gigantic Irishman, who had got a grant of a few hundred acres in the mountains, and had taken to himself a Scotch wife from among the free immigrants. The story ran that he was too busy to go to town, but asked a friend to go and pick a wife for him, "a fine shtrappin' woman, wid a good brisket on her."

The Doyles were large, slow, heavy men, with an instinct for the management of cattle; they were easily distinguished from the Donohoes, who were little red-whiskered men, enterprising and quick-witted, and ready to do anything in the world for a good horse. Other strangers and outlanders came to settle in the district, but from the original settlement up to the date of our story the two great families of the Doyles and the Donohoes governed the neighbourhood, and the headquarters of the clans was at Donohoe's "Shamrock Hotel," at Kiley's Crossing. Here they used to *rendezvous* when they went away down to the plains country each year for the shearing; for they added to their resources by travelling about the country shearing, droving, fencing, tanksinking, or doing any other job that offered itself, but always returned to their mountain fastnesses ready for any bit of work "on the cross" (i.e., unlawful) that might turn up. When times got hard they had a handy knack of finding horses that nobody had lost, shearing sheep they did not own, and branding and selling other people's calves.

When they stole stock, they moved them on through the mountains as quickly as possible, always having a brother or uncle, or a cousin—Terry or Timothy or Martin or Patsy—who had a holding "beyant." By these means they could shift stolen stock across the great range, and dispose of them among the peaceable folk who dwelt in the good country on the other side, whose stock they stole in return. Many a good horse and fat beast had made the stealthy mountain journey, lying hidden in gaps and gullies when pursuit grew hot, and being moved on as things quieted down.

Another striking feature was the way in which they got themselves mixed up with each other. Their names were so tangled up that no one could keep tally of them. There was a Red Mick Donohoe (son of the old publican), and his cousin Black Mick Donohoe, and Red Mick's son Mick, and Black Mick's son Mick, and Red Mick's son Pat, and Black Mick's son Pat; and there was Gammy Doyle (meaning Doyle with the lame leg), and Scrammy Doyle (meaning Doyle with the injured arm), and Bosthoon Doyle and Omadhaun Doyle—a Bosthoon being a man who never had any great amount of sense to speak of, while an Omadhaun is a man who began life with some sense, but lost most of it on his journey. It was a common saying in the country-side that if you met a man on the mountains you should say, "Good-day, Doyle," and if he replied, "That's not my name," you should at once say, "Well, I meant no offence, Mr. Donohoe."

One could generally pick which was which of the original stock, but when they came to intermarry there was no telling t'other from which. Startling likenesses cropped up among the relatives, and it was widely rumoured that one Doyle who was known to be in jail, and who was vaguely spoken of by the clan as being "away," was in fact serving an accumulation of sentences for himself and other members of the family, whose sins he had for a consideration taken on himself.

With such neighbours as these fighting him for every block of land, Andrew Gordon soon came to the end of his resources, and it was then that he had to take in his old manager as a partner. Before Bully Grant had been in the firm long, he had secured nearly all the good land, and the industrious yeomanry that the Land Act was supposed to create were hiding away up the gullies on miserable little patches of bad land, stealing sheep for a living. Bully fought them stoutly, impounded their sheep and cattle, and prosecuted trespassers and thieves; and, his luck being wonderful, he soon added to the enormous fortune he had made in mining, while Andrew Gordon died impoverished. When he died, old Bully gave the management of the stations to his sons, and contented himself with finding fault. But one dimly-remembered episode in his career was talked of by the old hands around Kiley's Hotel, long after Grant had become a wealthy man, and had gone for long trips to England.

Grant, in spite of the judgment and sagacity on which he prided himself, had at various times in his career made mistakes—mistakes in station management, mistakes about stock, mistakes about men, and last, but not least, mistakes about women; and it was to one of these mistakes that the gossips referred.

When he was a young man working as Mr. Gordon's manager, and living with the horse-breaker and the ration-carrier on the out-station at Kuryong (in those days a wild, half-civilised place), he had for neighbours Red Mick's father and mother, the original Mr. and Mrs. Donohoe, and their family. Their eldest daughter, Peggy—"Carrotty Peg," her relations called her—was at that time a fine, strapping, bush girl, and the only unmarried white woman anywhere near the station. She was as fair-complexioned as Red Mick himself, with a magnificent head of red hair, and the bust and limbs of a young Amazon.

This young woman, as she grew up, attracted the attention of Billy the Bully, and they used to meet a good deal out in the bush. On such occasions, he would possibly be occupied in the inspiring task of dragging a dead sheep after his horse, to make a trail to lead the wild dogs up to some poisoned meat; while the lady, clad in light and airy garments, with a huge white sunbonnet for head-gear, would be riding straddle-legged in search of strayed cows. When Grant left the station, and went away to make his fortune in mining, it was, perhaps, just a coincidence that this magnificent young creature grew tired of the old place and "cleared out," too. She certainly went away and disappeared so utterly that even her own people did not know what had become of her; to the younger generation her very existence was only a vague tradition. But it was whispered here and muttered there among the Doyles and the Donohoes and their friends and relations, that old Billy the Bully, on one of his visits to the interior, had been married to this undesirable lady by a duly accredited parson, in the presence of responsible witnesses; and that, when everyone had their own, Carrotty Peg, if alive, would be the lady of Kuryong. However, she had never come back to prove it, and no one cared about asking her alleged husband any unpleasant questions.

So much for the history of its owners; now to describe the homestead itself. It had originally consisted of the two-roomed slab hut, which had been added to from time to time. Kitchen, outhouses, bachelors' quarters, saddle-rooms, and store-rooms had been built on in a kind of straggling quadrangle, with many corners and unexpected doorways and passages; and it is reported that a swagman once got his dole of rations at the kitchen, went away, and after turning two or three corners, got so tangled up that when Fate led him back to the kitchen he didn't recognise it, and asked for rations over again, in the firm belief that he was at a different part of the house.

The original building was still the principal living-room, but the house had grown till it contained about twenty rooms. The slab walls had been plastered and whitewashed, and a wide verandah ran all along the front. Round the house were acres of garden, with great clumps of willows and acacias, where the magpies sat in the heat of the day and sang to one another in their sweet, low warble.

The house stood on a spur running from the hills. Looking down the river from it, one saw level flats waving with long grasses, in which the solemn cattle waded knee-deep. Here and there clumps of willows and stately poplars waved in the breeze. In the clear, dry air all colours were startlingly vivid, and round the nearer foothills wonderful lights and shadows played and shifted, while sometimes a white fleece of mist would drift slowly across a distant hill, like a film of snowy lace on the face of a beautiful woman. Away behind the foothills were the grand old mountains, with their snow-clad tops gleaming in the sun.

The garden was almost as lacking in design as the house. There were acres of fruit trees, with prairie grass growing at their roots, trees whereon grew luscious peaches and juicy egg-plums; long vistas of grapevines, with little turnings and alleys, regular lovers' walks, where the scent of honeysuckle intoxicated the senses. At the foot of the garden was the river, a beautiful stream, fed by the mountain-snow, and rushing joyously over clear gravel beds, whose million-tinted pebbles dashed in the sunlight like so many opals.

In some parts of Australia it is difficult to tell summer from winter; but up in this mountain-country each season had its own attractions. In the spring the flats were green with lush grass, speckled with buttercups and bachelors' buttons, and the willows put out their new leaves, and all manner of shy dry-scented bush flowers bloomed on the ranges; and the air was full of the song of birds and the calling of animals. Then came summer, when never a cloud decked the arch of blue sky, and all animated nature drew into the shade of big trees until the evening breeze sprang up, bringing sweet scents of the dry grass and ripening grain. In autumn, the leaves of the English trees turned all tints of yellow and crimson, and the grass in the paddocks went brown; and the big bullock teams worked from dawn till dark, hauling in their loads of hay from the cultivation paddocks.

But most beautiful of all was winter, when logs blazed in the huge fireplaces, and frosts made the ground crisp, and the stock, long-haired and shaggy, came snuffling round the stables, picking up odds and ends of straw; when the grey, snow-clad mountains looked but a stone's throw away in the intensely clear air, and the wind brought a colour to the cheeks and a tingling to the blood that made life worth living.

Such was Kuryong homestead, where lived Charlie Gordon's mother and his brother Hugh, with a lot of children left by another brother who, like many others, had gone up to Queensland to make his fortune, and had left his bones there instead; and to look after these young folk there was a governess, Miss Harriott.

CHAPTER V
THE COMING OF THE HEIRESS

The spring—the glorious hill-country spring—was down on Kuryong. All the flats along Kiley's River were knee-deep in green grass. The wattle-trees were out in golden bloom, and the snow-water from the mountains set the river running white with foam, fighting its way over bars of granite into big pools where the platypus dived, and the wild ducks—busy with the cares of nesting—just settled occasionally to snatch a hasty meal and then hurried off, with a whistle of strong wings, back to their little ones. The breeze brought down from the hills a scent of grass and bush flowers. There was life and movement everywhere. The little foals raced and played all day in the sunshine round their big sleepy mothers; the cattle bellowed to each other from hill to hill; even those miserable brutes, the sheep, frisked in an ungainly way when anything startled them. At all the little mountain-farms and holdings young Doyles and Donohoes were catching their horses, lean after the winter's starvation, and loading the pack-saddles for their five-months' trip out to the borders of Queensland, from shearing-shed to shearing-shed. A couple of months before they started, they would write to the squatters for whom they had worked on previous shearings— such quaint, ill-spelled letters—asking that a pen might be kept for them. Great shearers they were, too, for the mountain air bred hardy men, and while they were at it they worked feverishly, bending themselves nearly double over the sheep, and making the shears fly till the sweat ran down their foreheads and dripped on the ground; and they peeled the yellow wool off sheep after sheep as an expert cook peels an apple. In the settled districts such as Kuryong, where the flocks were small, they were made to shear carefully; but away out on the Queensland side, on a station with two hundred thousand sheep to get through, they rushed the wool off savagely. He was a poor specimen of the clan who couldn't shear his hundred and twenty sheep between bell and bell; and the price was a pound a hundred, with plenty of stations wanting shearers, so they made good cheques in those days.

One glorious spring morning, Hugh Gordon was sitting in his office— every squatter and station-manager has an office—waiting with considerable impatience the coming of the weekly mail. The office looked like a blend of stationer's shop, tobacconist's store, and saddlery warehouse. A row of pigeon-holes along the walls was filled with letters and papers; the rafters were hung with saddles and harness; a tobacco-cutter and a jar of tobacco stood on the table, side by side with some formidable-looking knives, used for cutting the sheep's feet when they became diseased; whips and guns stood in every corner; nails and saws filled up a lot of boxes on the table, and a few samples of wool hung from a rope that was stretched across the room. The mantelpiece was occupied by bottles of horse-medicine and boxes of cartridges; an elderly white cockatoo, chained by the leg to a galvanised iron perch, sunned himself by the door, and at intervals gave an exhibition of his latest accomplishment, in which he imitated the yowl of a trodden-on cat much better than the cat could have done it himself.

The air was heavy with scent. All round the great quadrangle of the house acacia trees were in bloom, and the bees were working busily among the mignonette and roses in front of the office door.

Hugh Gordon was a lithe, wiry young Australian with intensely sunburnt face and hands, and a drooping black moustache; a man with a healthy, breezy outdoor appearance, but the face of an artist, a dreamer, and a thinker, rather than that of a practical man. His brother Charlie and he, though very much alike in face, were quite different types of manhood. Charlie, from his earliest school-days, had never read a book except under compulsion, had never stayed indoors when he could possibly get out, had never obeyed an unwelcome order when by force or fraud he could avoid doing so, and had never written a letter in his life when a telegram would do. He took the world as it came, having no particular amount of imagination, and never worried himself. Hugh, on the other hand, was inclined to meet trouble half-way, and to make troubles where none existed, which is the worst misfortune that a man can be afflicted with.

Hugh walked to the door and gazed out over the garden and homestead, down the long stretch of green paddocks where fat cattle were standing under the trees, too well fed to bother themselves with looking for grass. He looked beyond all this to the long drab-coloured stretch of road that led to Kiley's, watching for the mailboy's arrival. The mail was late, for the melting snow had flooded the mountain creeks, and Hugh knew it was quite likely that little Patsy Donohoe, the mail-boy, had been blocked at Donohoe's Hotel for two days, unable to cross Kiley's River. This had happened often, and on various occasions when Patsy had crossed, he, pony and all, had been swept down quite a quarter of a mile in the ice-cold water before they could reach land. But that was an ordinary matter in the spring, and it was a point of honour with Patsy and all his breed not to let the elements beat them in carrying out the mail contract, which they tendered for every year, and in which no outsider would have dared to compete.

At last Hugh's vigil was rewarded by the appearance of a small and wild-looking boy, mounted on a large and wild-looking horse. The boy was about twelve years of age, and had just ridden a half-broken horse a forty-mile journey—for of such is the youth of Australia. Patsy was wet and dirty, and the big leather mail-bag that he handed over had evidently been under water.

"We had to swim, Mr. Hugh," the boy said triumphantly, "and this great, clumsy cow" (the child referred to his horse), "he reared over on me in the water, twyst, but I stuck to him. My oath!"

Hugh laughed. "I expect Kiley's River will get you yet, Patsy," he said. "Go in now to the kitchen and get dry by the fire. I'll lend you a horse to get back on to-morrow. You can camp here till then, there's no hurry back."

The boy let his horse go loose, dismissing it with a parting whack on the rump with the bridle, and swaggered inside, carrying his saddle, to show his wet clothes and recount his deeds to the admiring cook. Patsy was not one to hide his light under a bushel.

Hugh carried the bag into the office, and shook out the letters and papers on the table. Everything was permeated with a smell of wet leather, and some of the newspapers were rather pulpy. After sending out everybody else's mail he turned to examine his own. Out of the mass of letters, agents' circulars, notices of sheep for sale, catalogues of city firms, and circulars from pastoral societies, he picked a letter addressed to himself in the scrawling fist of William Grant. He opened it, expecting to find in it the usual Commination Service on things in general, but as he read on, a vivid surprise spread over his face. Leaving the other letters and papers unopened, he walked to the door and looked out into the courtyard, where Stuffer, the youngest of his nephews, who was too small to be allowed to join in the field sports of the others, was playing at being a railway train. He had travelled in a train once, and now passed Hugh's door under easy steam, working his arms and legs like piston-rods, and giving piercing imitations of a steam-whistle at intervals.

"Stuffer," said Hugh, "do you know where your grandmother is?"

"No" said the Stuffer laconically. "I don't Choo, choo, choo, Whee-aw!"

"Well, look here," said Hugh, "you just railway-train yourself round the house till you find her, and let me know where she is. I want to see her. Off you go now."

The Stuffer steamed himself out with the action of an engine drawing a long train of cars, and disappeared round the corner of the house.

Before long he was back, drew himself up alongside an imaginary platform, intimated that his grandmother was in the verandah, and then proceeded to let the steam hiss out of his safety-valve.

Hugh walked across the quadrangle, under the acacia tree, heavy with blossoms, in which a myriad bees were droning at their work, and through the house on to the front verandah, which looked over the wide sweep of river-flat. Here he found his mother and Miss Harriott, the governess, peeling apples for dumplings—great rosy-checked, solid-fleshed apples, that the hill-country turns out in perfection. The old lady was slight in figure, with a refined face, and a carriage erect in spite of her years. Miss Harriott was of a languid Spanish type, with black eyes and strongly-marked eyebrows. She had a *petite*, but well-rounded figure, with curiously small hands and feet. Though only about twenty-four years of age she had the sedate and unemotional look that one sees in doctors and nurses—people who have looked on death and birth, and sorrow and affliction. For Ellen Harriott had done her three years' course as a nurse; she had a natural faculty for the business, and was in great request among the wild folk of the mountains, who looked upon her (and perhaps rightly) as quite equal to the Tarrong doctor in any emergency. She knew them all, for she had lived nearly all her life at Kuryong. When the family moved there from the back country a tutor was needed for the boys, and an old broken-down gentleman accepted the billet at low pay, on condition that he was allowed to bring his little daughter with him. When he died, the daughter still stayed on, and was made governess to the new generation of young folk. She was a queer, self-contained girl, saying little; and as Hugh walked in, she looked up at him, and wondered what new trouble was bringing him to his mother with the open letter in his hand.

"Mother," said Hugh, "I have had a most extraordinary letter."

"From Mr. Grant?" said the old lady, "What does he say?"

She saw by her son's face that there was something more than usual in the wind, but one who had lived her life, from fortune to poverty, through strife and trial, was prepared to take things much more easily than Hugh.

"Is it anything very serious?"

"His daughter's coming out to live here."

"What?"

"Yes, here's the letter. It only came this morning. Patsy was late, the river is up. I'll read it to you."

Seating himself at the table, Hugh spread out the letter, and read it:—

Dear Gordon,

The last lot of wethers, though they topped the market, only realised 10/-. I think you would show better judgment in keeping these sheep back a little. Don't rely upon Satton's advice. He is generally wrong, and is always most wrong when he is most sure he is right.

My daughter has arrived from England, and will at once go up to the station. I have written to your mother on the subject. My daughter will represent me in everything, so I wish her to learn a little about stations. Send to meet her at the train on Wednesday next.

Yours truly,
W. G. GRANT.

"Wednesday next!" said Hugh, "that letter is three days delayed. Patsy couldn't cross the river. She'll be there before we can possibly get down. If no one meets her I wonder if she'll have pluck enough to get into the coach and come on to Donohoe's."

"I don't envy her the trip, if she does," said Miss Harriott. "The coach-drive over those roads will seem awful to an English girl."

"I'll have to go down at once, anyhow," said Hugh, "and meet her on the road somewhere. If she is at the railway, I can get there in two days. Have you a letter, Mother?"

"Yes," said the old lady, "but I won't show it to you now. You shall see it some other time."

"Well, I'll set about making a start," said Hugh. "What trap had I better take?"

"You'd better take the big waggonette," said the old lady, in her soft voice. "A young girl just out from England is sure to have a great deal of luggage, you know. I wonder if she is anything like Mr. Grant. I hope her temper is a little bit better."

"You'd better come down with me, Miss Harriott, to meet her," said Hugh. "I don't suppose your luggage would be a load there and back, anyhow."

"What about crossing the river?" said the old lady.

"Oh, we'll get across somehow," said Hugh, "will you come?"

"I think I'll wait," said the young lady meditatively, "She'll be tired from travelling and looking after her luggage, and she had better meet the family one at a time. You go and meet her, and your mother and I will get her room ready. Does the letter say any more about her?"

"No, that's all," said Hugh. "Well, I'll send the boy to run in the horses. I'll take four horses in the big waggonette; I expect she'll be waiting at Donohoe's—that is, if she left the railway-station in the coach—if she is at Donohoe's I'll be back before dark."

With this he went back to the office, and his mother and Miss Harriott went their separate ways to prepare for the comfort of the heiress. To Ellen Harriott the arrival was a new excitement, a change in the monotony of bush life; but to the old lady and Hugh it meant a great deal more. It meant that they would be no longer master and mistress of the big station on which they had lived so long, and which was now so much under their control that it seemed almost like their own.

Everything depended on what the girl was like. They had never even seen a photograph of her, and awaited her coming in a state of nervous expectancy. All over the district they had been practically considered owners of the big station; Hugh had taken on and dismissed employees at his will, had controlled the buying and selling of thousands of sheep and cattle, and now this strange girl was to come in with absolute power over them. They would be servants and dependants on the station, which had once belonged to them.

After Hugh had gone, the old lady sat back in her armchair and read over again her letter from Mr. Grant; and, lest it should be thought that that gentleman had only one side to his character, it is as well for the reader to know what was in the letter. It ran as follows:—

Dear Mrs. Gordon,

> I am writing to you about a most important matter. Colonel Selwyn is dead, and my daughter has come out from England. I don't know anyone to take charge of her except yourself. I am an old man now, and set in my ways, and this girl is really all I have to live for. Looking back on my life, I see where I have been a fool; and perhaps the good fortune that has followed me has been more luck than anything else.

Your husband was a smarter man than I am, and he came to grief, though I will say that I always warned him against that Western place.

Do you remember the old days when we had the two little homesteads, and I used to ride down from the out-station of a Saturday and spend Sunday with you and Andrew, and talk over the fortunes we were going to make? If I had met a woman like you in those days I might have been a better man. As it was, I made a fool of myself. But that's all past praying for.

Now about my girl. If you will take her, and make her as good a woman as yourself, or as near it as you can, you will earn my undying thanks. As to money matters, when I die she will of course have a great deal of money, so that it is well she should begin now to learn how to use it; I have, therefore, given her full power to draw all money that may be required. I may tell you that I intend to leave your boys enough to start them in life, and they will have a first-class chance to get on. I am sending Charlie out to the West, to take over a block which those fools, Sutton and Co., got me to advance money on, and on which the man cannot pay his interest. He will be away for some time.

Meanwhile, dear Mrs. Gordon, for the sake of old times, do what you can for the girl. I expect she has been brought up with English ideas. I can't get her to say much to me, which I daresay is my own fault. After she has been with you for a bit, I will come up and stay for a time at the station.

Yours very truly,
W. G. GRANT.

Reading this letter called back the whole panorama of the past—the old days when she and her husband were struggling in the rough, hard, pioneering life, and the blacks were thick round the station; the birth of her children, and the ups and downs of her husband's fortunes; then the burial of her husband out on the sandhills, and her flight to this haven of rest at Kuryong. Though she had lost interest in things for herself, she felt keenly for her children, and was sick at heart when she thought what this girl, who was to wield such power over them, might turn out to be. But she hoped that Grant's daughter, whatever else she might be, would at any rate be a genuine, straight-forward girl; and filled with this hope, she sat down to answer him:

> "Dear Mr. Grant," she wrote, "I have received your letter. Hugh has gone down to meet your daughter, but the mails were delayed owing to the river being up, and he may not get to the railway station as soon as she arrives. I will do what I can for her, and I thank you for what you say you will do for my boys. I will let you know the moment she arrives. I wish you would come up and live on the station for a time. It would be better for you than life in the club, without a friend to care for you. If ever you feel inclined to stay here for a time, I hope you will at once let me know. With thanks and best wishes,
>
> Yours truly,
ANNETTE GORDON."

CHAPTER VI
A COACH ACCIDENT

The coach from Tarrong railway station to Emu Flat, and then on to Donohoe's Hotel, ran twice a week. Pat Donohoe was mailman, contractor and driver, and his admirers said that Pat could hit his five horses in more places at once than any other man on the face of the earth. His coach was horsed by the neighbouring squatters, through whose stations the road ran; and any horse that developed homicidal tendencies, or exhibited a disinclination to work, was at once handed over to the mailman to be licked into shape. The result was that, as a rule, Pat was driving teams composed of animals that would do anything but go straight, but under his handling they were generally persuaded, after a day or two, to settle down to their work.

On the day when Hugh and Mrs. Gordon read Mr. Grant's letter at Kuryong, the train deposited at Tarrong a self-reliant young lady of about twenty, accompanied by nearly a truck-full of luggage—solid leather portmanteaux, canvas-covered bags, iron boxes, and so on—which produced a great sensation among the rustics. She was handsome enough to be called a beauty, and everything about her spoke of exuberant health and vitality. Her figure was supple, and she had the clear pink and white complexion which belongs to cold climates.

She seemed accustomed to being waited on, and watched without emotion the guard and the solitary railway official—porter, station-master, telegraph-operator and lantern-man, all rolled into one—haul her hundredweights of luggage out of the train. Then she told the perspiring station-master, etc., to please have the luggage sent to the hotel, and marched over to that building in quite an assured way, carrying a small handbag. Three commercial travellers, who had come up by the same train, followed her off the platform, and the most gallant of the three winked at his friends, and then stepped up and offered to carry her bag. The young lady gave him a pleasant smile, and handed him the bag; together they crossed the street, while the other commercials marched disconsolately behind. At the door of the hotel she took the bag from her cavalier, and there and then, in broad Australian daylight, rewarded him with twopence—a disaster which caused him to apply to his firm for transfer to some foreign country at once. She marched into the bar, where Dan, the landlord's son, was sweeping, while Mrs. Connellan, the landlady, was wiping glasses in the midst of a stale fragrance of overnight beer and tobacco-smoke.

"I am going to Kuryong," said the young lady, "and I expected to meet Mr. Gordon here. Is he here?"

Mrs. Connellan looked at her open-eyed. Such an apparition was not often seen in Tarrong. Mr. and Mrs. Connellan had only just "taken the pub.", and what with trying to keep Connellan sober and refusing drinks to tramps, loafers, and black-fellows, Mrs. Connellan was pretty well worn out. As for making the hotel pay, that idea had been given up long ago. It was against Mrs. Connellan's instincts of hospitality to charge anyone for a meal or a bed, and when any great rush of bar trade took place it generally turned out to be "Connellan's shout," so the hotel was not exactly a goldmine. In fact, Mrs. Connellan had decided that the less business she did, the more money she would make; and she rather preferred that people should not stop at her hotel. This girl looked as if she would give trouble; might even expect clean beds and clean sheets when there were none within the hotel, and might object to fleas, of which there were plenty. So the landlady pulled herself together, and decided to speed the parting guest as speedily as possible.

"Mr. Gordon couldn't git in," she said. "The cricks (creeks) is all up. The coach is going down to Kiley's Crossing to-day. You had better go with that."

"How soon does the coach start?"

"In an hour or two. As soon as Pat Donohoe, the mailman, has got a horse shod. Come in and have a wash, and fix yourself up till breakfast is ready. Where's your bag?"

"My luggage is at the railway-station."

"I'll send Dan over for it. Dan, Dan, Dan!"

"'Ello," said Dan's voice, from the passage, where, with the wild-eyed servant-girl, he had been taking stock of the new arrival.

"Go over to the station and git this lady's bag. Is there much to carry?"

"There are only four portmanteaux and three bags, and two boxes and a hat-box, and a roll of rugs; and please be careful of the hat-box."

"You'd better git the barrer, Dan."

"Better git the bloomin' bullock-dray," growled Dan, quite keen to see this aggregation of luggage; and foreseeing something to talk about for the next three months. "She must ha' come up to start a store, I reckon," said Dan; and off he went to struggle with boxes for the next half-hour or so.

Over Mary Grant's experiences at the Tarrong Hotel we will not linger. The dirty water, peopled by wriggling animalculae, that she poured out of the bedroom jug; the damp, cloudy, unhealthy-smelling towel on which she dried her face; the broken window through which she could hear herself being discussed by loafers in the yard; all these things are matters of course in bush townships, for the Australian, having a soul above details, does not shine at hotel-keeping. The breakfast was enlivened by snatches of song from the big, good-natured bush-girl who waited at table, and who "fancied" her voice somewhat, and marched into the breakfast-room singing in an ear-splitting Soprano:

"It's a vilet from me"—

(*spoken.*) "What you'll have, there's chops, steaks, and bacon and eggs"—"Chops, please."

(*singer continues.*) "Sainted mother's"—

(*spoken.*) "Tea or coffee"—"Tea, please."

(*singer finishes.*)—"grave."

While she ate, Miss Grant had an uneasy feeling that she was being stared at; all the female staff and hangers-on of the place having gathered round the door to peer in at her and to appraise to the last farthing her hat, her tailor-made gown, and her solid English walking-shoes, and to indulge in wild speculation as to who or what she could be. A Kickapoo Indian in full war-paint, arriving suddenly in a little English village, could not have created more excitement than she did at Tarrong. After breakfast she walked out on the verandah that ran round the little one-story weatherboard hotel, and looked down the mile and a-half of road, with little galvanised-iron-roofed cottages at intervals of a quarter of a mile or so, that constituted the township. She watched Conroy, the policeman, resplendent in breeches and polished boots, swagger out from the court-house yard, leading his horse to water. The town was waking to its daily routine; Garry, the butcher, took down the clumsy board that passed for a window-shutter, and McDermott, the carter, passed the hotel, riding a huge rough-coated draught-horse, bare-backed. Everyone gave him a "Mornin', Billy!" as he passed, and he returned the greeting as he did every morning of his life. A few children loitered past to the little school-house, staring at her as though she were some animal.

She was in a hurry to get away—English people always are—but in the bright lexicon of the bush there is no such word as hurry. Tracey, the blacksmith, had not by any means finished shoeing the coach-horse yet. So Mrs. Connellan made an attempt to find out who she was, and why she was going to Kuryong.

"You'll have a nice trip in the coach," she said. "Lier (lawyer) Blake's going down. He's a nice feller."

"Yes?"

"Father Kelly, too. He's good company."

"Yes?"

"Are you staying long at Kuryong?"

"Some time, I expect."

"Are you going to teach the children?"

"No, I'm going to live there. My father owns Kuryong. My father is Mr. Grant."

Mrs. Connellan was simply staggered at this colossal treasure-trove, this majestic piece of gossip that had fallen on her like rain from Heaven. Mr. Grant's daughter! Going out to Kuryong! What a piece of news! Hardly knowing what she did, she shuffled out of the room, and interrupted the singing waitress who was wiping plates, and had just got back to "It's a vilet" when Mrs. Connellan burst in on her.

"Maggie! Maggie! Do you know who that is? Grant's daughter! The one that used to be in England. She must be going to Kuryong to live, with all that luggage. What'll the Gordons say? The old lady won't like it, will she? This'll be a bit of news, won't it?" And she went off to tell the cook, while Maggie darted to the door to meet Dan, and tell him.

Dan told the station-master when he went back for the next load, and when he had finished carting the luggage he got on a horse and went round telling everybody in the little town. The station-master told the ganger of the four navvies who went by on their trolly down the line to work. At the end of their four-mile length they told the ration-carrier of Eubindal station, who happened to call in at their camp for a drink of tea. He hurried off to the head-station with the news, and on his way told three teamsters, an inspector of selections, and a black boy belonging to Mylong station, whom he happened to meet on the road. Each of them told everybody that they met, pulling up and standing in their stirrups to discuss the matter in all its bearings, in the leisurely style of the bush; and wondering what she had come out for, whether the Gordons would get the sack from Kuryong, whether she would marry Hugh Gordon, whether she was engaged already, whether she was good-looking, how much money she had, and how much old Grant would leave her. In fact, before twenty-four hours were over, all the district knew of her arrival; which possibly explains how news travels in Africa among the Kaffirs, who are supposed to have a signalling system that no one has yet fathomed; but the way it gets round in Australia is just as wonderful as among the Kaffirs, in fact, for speed and thoroughness of information we should be inclined to think that our coloured brethren run a bad second.

At last, however, Tracey had finished shoeing the coach-horse, and Miss Grant, with part of her luggage, took a seat on the coach behind five of Donohoe's worst horses, next to a well-dressed, powerfully-built man of about five-and-twenty. He looked and talked like a gentleman, and she heard the coachman address him as "Mr. Blake." She and he shared the box-seat with the driver, and just at the last moment the local priest hurried up and climbed on the coach. In some unaccountable way he had missed hearing who the young lady was, and for a time he could only look at her back-hair and wonder.

It was not long before, in the free and easy Australian style, the passengers began to talk to each other as the coach bumped along its monotonous road—up one hill, through an avenue of dusty, tired-looking gum-trees, down the other side through a similar avenue, up another hill precisely the same as the last, and so on.

Blake was the first to make advances. "Not much to be seen on this sort of journey, Miss Grant," he said.

The young lady looked at him with serious eyes. "No," she said, "we've only seen two houses since we left the town. All the rest of the country seems to be a wilderness."

Here the priest broke in. He was a broth of a boy from Maynooth, just the man to handle the Doyle and Donohoe congregation.

"It's the big stations is the roon of the country," he said. "How is the country to go ahead at all wid all the good land locked up? There's Kuryong on ahead here would support two hundthred fam'lies, and what does it employ now? Half a dozen shepherds, widout a rag to their back."

"I am going to Kuryong," said the girl; and the priest was silent.

By four in the afternoon they reached Kiley's River, running yellow and froth-covered with melting snow. The coachman pulled his horses up on the bank, and took a good, long look at the bearings. As they waited, the Kuryong vehicle came down on the other side of the river.

"There's Mr. Gordon," said the coachman. "I don't think he'll try it. I reckon it's a trifle deep for me. Do you want to get across particular, Mr. Blake?"

"Yes, very particularly, Pat. I've told Martin Donohoe to meet me down here with some witnesses in a cattle-stealing case."

"What about you, Father Kelly?"

"I'm go'n on to Tim Murphy's dyin' bed. Put 'em into the wather, they'll take it aisy."

The driver turned to the third passenger. "It's a bit dangerous-like, Miss. If you like to get out, it's up to you to say so. The coach might wash over. There's a settler's place up the river a mile. You can go and stay there till the river goes down, and Mr. Gordon 'll come and meet you."

"Thanks, I'll go on," said the lady.

Preparations for crossing the river were soon made. Anything that would spoil by getting wet, or that would float out of the coach, was lifted up and packed on the roof. The passengers stood up on the seats. Then Pat Donohoe put the whip on his leaders, and calling to his two wheelers, old-seasoned veterans, he put them at it.

Snorting and trembling, the leaders picked their way into the yellow water, the coach bumping over the rubble of the crossing-place. Hugh Gordon, watching from the far-side of the river, saw the coach dip and rock and plunge over the boulders. On it came till the water was actually lapping into the body of the coach, roaring and swirling round the horses' legs, up to their flanks and bellies, while the driver called out to them and kept them straight with voice and reins. Every spring he had a similar crossing, and he knew almost to an inch at what height it was safe to go into the river. But this time, as ill-luck would have it, the off-side leader was a young, vicious, thorough-bred colt, who had been handed over to him to be cured of a propensity for striking people with his fore-feet. As the horses worked their way into the river, the colt, with the courage of his breeding, pulled manfully, and breasted the current fearlessly. But suddenly a floating log drifted down, and struck him on the front legs. In an instant he reared up, and threw himself heavily sideways against his mate, bringing him to his knees; then the two of them, floundering and scrambling, were borne away with the current, dragging the coach after them. In a few yards they were off the causeway; the coach, striking deep water, settled like a boat, and turned over on its side, with the leaders swimming for their lives. As for the wheelers, they were pulled down with the vehicle, and were almost drowning in their harness.

Cool as a cucumber, Blake had turned to the girl. "Can you swim?" he said. And she answered him as cooly, "Yes, a little."

"Well, put your hands on my shoulders, and leave everything to me." Just then the coach settled over with one final surge, and they were in the water.

Away they went with the roaring current, the girl clinging fast to his shoulders, while he gave his whole attention to dodging the stumps and snags that were showing their formidable teeth above water. For a while she was able to hold on. Then, with a sickening sense of helplessness, she felt herself torn from him, and whirled away like a leaf. The rank smell of the muddy water was in her nostrils, the fear of death in her heart. She struggled to keep afloat. Suddenly a blood-streaked face appeared, and Blake, bleeding from a cut on the forehead, caught her with a strong grip and drew her to him. A few more seconds of whirling chaos, and she felt land under her feet, and Blake half-carrying her to the bank. They had been swept on to one of the many sand-banks which ran out into the stream, and were safe.

Half-hysterical, she sat down on a huge log, and waited while Blake ran up-stream to give help to the coachman. While the two had been battling in the water, the priest had stayed with the coachman to cut the horses free, till at last all four got clear of the wreck, and swam ashore. Then the men followed them, drifting down the current and fighting their way to shore at about the same place.

Hugh Gordon drove the waggonette down to pick up the party when they landed. The scene on the bank would have made a good picture. The horses, dripping with water and shaking with cold, were snorting and staring, while the coachman was trying to fix up some gear out of the wreck, so that he could ride one of them. The priest, his broad Irish face ornamented by a black clay pipe, was tramping up and down in his wet clothes. Blake was helping Miss Grant to wring the water out of her clothes, and she was somewhat incoherently trying to thank him. As Hugh drove up, Blake looked up and caught his eye, and there flashed between the two men an unmistakable look of hostility. Then Hugh jumped from the waggonette, and walked up to Miss Grant, holding out his hand.

"I'm Hugh Gordon," he said. "We only got your father's letter to-day, or I would have been down to meet you. I hope you are not hurt. Jump into the trap, and I'll run down to the Donohoes', and get you some dry things." Then, turning to Blake, he said somewhat stiffly, "Will you get in, Mr. Blake?"

"Thanks," said Blake, equally stiffly, "I can ride one of the mail horses. It's no distance. I wont trouble you."

But the girl turned and put her hand into Blake's, and spoke with the air of a queen.

"I am very much obliged to you—more than I can tell you. You have saved my life. If ever I can do anything to repay you I will."

"Oh, nonsense," said Blake, "that's nothing. It was only a matter of dodging the stumps. You'd better get on now to Donohoe's Hotel, and get Mrs. Donohoe to find some dry things for you."

The mere fact of his refusing a lift showed that there was some hostility between himself and Hugh Gordon; but the priest, who had climbed into the Kuryong vehicle as a matter of course, settled the matter off-hand.

"Get in the trap," he said. "Get in the trap, man. What's the use for two of ye to ride the mail horses, and get your death o' cold? Get in the trap!"

"Of course I'll give you a lift," said Hugh. "Jump in, and let us get away before you all get colds. What will you do about the coach and the luggage, Pat?"

"I'll borry them two old draught horses from Martin Donohoe, and they'll haul it out. Bedad, some o' that luggage 'll be washed down to the Murrumbidgee before night; but the most of it is strapped on. Push along, Mr. Gordon, and tell Martin I'm coming."

With some reluctance Blake got into the waggonette; before long they were at Donohoe's Hotel, and Mary Grant was soon rigged out in an outfit from Mrs. Donohoe's best clothes—a pale-green linsey bodice and purple skirt—everything, including Mrs. Donohoe's boots, being about four sizes too big. But she looked by no means an unattractive little figure, with her brown eyes and healthy colour showing above the shapeless garments.

She came into the little sitting-room laughing at the figure she cut, sat down, and drank scalding tea, and ate Mrs. Donohoe's cakes, while talking with Father Kelly and Blake over the great adventure.

When she was ready to start she got into the waggonette alongside Hugh, and waved good-bye to the priest and Blake and Mrs. Donohoe, as though they were old friends. She had had her first touch of colonial experience.

CHAPTER VII
MR. BLAKE'S RELATIONS

As soon as Hugh got his team swinging along at a steady ten miles an hour on the mountain road, Mary Grant opened the conversation.

"Mr. Gordon," she said, "who is Mr. Blake?"

"He's the lawyer from Tarrong."

"Yes, I know. Mrs. Connellan called him the 'lier.' But I thought you didn't seem to like him. Isn't he nice?"

"I suppose so. His father was a gentleman—the police magistrate up here."

"Then, why don't you like him? Is there anything wrong about him?"

Hugh straightened his leaders and steadied the vehicle over a little gully.

"There's nothing wrong about him," he said, "only—his mother was one of the Donohoes—not a lady, you know—and he always goes with those people; and, of course, that means he doesn't go much with us."

"Why not?"

"Well, you see, they're selectors, and they look on the station people as—well, rather against them, you know—sort of enemies—and he has never come to the station. But there is no reason why he shouldn't."

"He saved my life," said Mary Grant.

"Certainly he did," said Hugh. "I'll say that for Blake, he fears nothing. One of the pluckiest men alive. And how did you feel? Were you much frightened?"

"Yes, horribly. I have often wondered whether I should be brave, you know, and now I don't think I am. Not the least bit. But Mr. Blake seemed so strong—directly he caught hold of me I felt quite safe, somehow. If you don't mind, I would like to ask him out to the station."

"Certainly, Miss Grant. My mother will only be too glad. She was sorry that we did not get down to meet you. The letter was delayed."

Mary Grant laughed as she looked down at Mrs. Donohoe's clothes. "What a sight I am!" she said.

"But, after all, it's Australia, isn't it? And I have had such adventures already! You know you will have to show me all about the station and the sheep and cattle. Will you do that?"

Hugh thought there was nothing in the world he would like better, but contented himself with a formal offer to teach her the noble art of squatting.

"You must begin at once and tell me things. What estate are we on now?" she asked.

"This is your father's station. All you can see around belongs to him; but after the next gate we come on some land held by selectors."

"Who are they?"

"Well," said Hugh, a little awkwardly, "they are relations of Mr. Blake's. You'll see what an Australian farmer's homestead is like."

They drove through a rickety wire-and-sapling gate and across about a mile of bush, and suddenly came on a little slab house nestling under the side of a hill. At the back were the stockyards and the killing-pen, where a contrivance for raising dead cattle—called a gallows—waved its arms to the sky. In front of the house there was rather a nice little garden. At the back were a lot of dilapidated sheds, leaning in all directions. A mob of sheep was penned in a yard outside one of the sheds; and in the garden an old woman, white-haired and wrinkled, with a very short dress showing a lot of dirty stocking and slipshod elastic-sided boot, was bending over a spade, digging potatoes.

The old woman straightened herself as they drove up.

"Good daah to you, Misther Gordon," she said. "Good daah to you, Miss."

"Good day, Mrs. Doyle," said Hugh. "Hard work that, this weather. How's all the family?"

"Mag—Marg'rut, I mane—she's inside. That's her playin' the pianny. She just got it up from Sydney."

"And where's Peter?"

"Peter's shearin' the sheep. He's in that shed there beyant. He's the only shearer we have, so we tell him he's the ringer of the shed. He works terr'ble hard, does Peter. He's not—" and the old woman dropped her voice—"he's not all there in the head, is Peter, you know."

"And where's Mick?"

"Mick, bad scran to him! He's bought a jumpin' haarse (horse), and he's gone to hell leppin! Down at one of the shows he is, some place. He has too much sense to work, has Mick. Won't you come in and have a cup of tay?"

"No, we must get on, thank you," and Hugh and Mary drove off, watched by the old lady and the lanky-legged, shock-headed youth—Peter himself—who came to the door of the big shed to stare at them.

As they drove off Hugh was silent, wondering what effect the sight of the selectors might have had on Miss Grant.

She seemed to read his thoughts, and after a little while she spoke.

"So those are Mr. Blake's poor relations, are they? Well, that is not his fault. My father was poor once, just as poor as those people are. And Mr. Blake saved my life."

Hugh felt that she was half-consciously putting him in the wrong for having more or less disapproved of Mr. Blake; so he kept silence.

As the team bore them along at a flying trot, they climbed higher and higher up the range; at last, as they rounded a shoulder of the hillside, the whole valley of Kiley's River lay beneath them, stretching away to the far blue foothills. Beyond again was a great mountain, its top streaked with snow. At their feet was a gorgeous scheme of colour, greens and greys of the grass, bright tints of willow and poplar, and the speckled forms of the cattle, so far down that they looked like pigmy stock feeding in fairy paddocks. Across the valley there came now and again, softened by distance, the song of the river; and up in the river-bend, on a spur of the hills, were white walls rising from clustered greenery.

"How beautiful!" said the girl, half standing up in the waggonette, "and is that—"

"That's Kuryong, Miss Grant. Your home station."

CHAPTER VIII
AT THE HOMESTEAD

Miss Grant's arrival at Kuryong homestead caused great excitement among the inhabitants. Mrs. Gordon received her in a motherly way, trying hard not to feel that a new mistress had come into the house; she was anxious to see whether the girl exhibited any signs of her father's fiery temper and imperious disposition. The two servant-girls at the homestead — great herculean, good-natured bush-girls, daughters of a boundary-rider, whose highest ideal of style and refinement was Kuryong drawing-room — breathed hard and stared round-eyed, like wild fillies, at the unconscious intruder. The station-hands — Joe, the wood-and-water boy, old Alfred the groom, Bill the horse-team driver, and Harry Warden the married man, who helped with sheep, mended fences, and did station-work in general — all watched for a sight of her. They exchanged opinions about her over their smoke at night by the huge open fireplace in the men's hut, where they sat in a semicircle, toasting their shins at the blaze till their trousers smoked again, each man with a pipe of black tobacco going full swing from tea till bedtime. But the person who felt the most intense excitement over the arrival of the heiress was Miss Harriott.

For all her nurse's experience, Ellen Harriott was not a woman of the world. Except for the period of her hospital training, she had passed all her life shut up among the mountains. Her dream-world was mostly constructed out of high-class novels, and she united a shrewd wit and a clever brain to a dense ignorance of the real world, that left her like a ship without a rudder. She was, like most bush-reared girls, a great visionary — many a castle-in-the-air had she built while taking her daily walk by the river under the drooping willows. The visions, curiously enough, always took the direction of magnificence. She pictured herself as a leader of society, covered with diamonds, standing at the head of a broad marble staircase and receiving Counts by the dozen (*vide* Ouida's novels, read by stealth); or else as a rich man's wife who dispensed hospitality regally, and was presented at Court, and set the fashion in dress and jewels. At the back of all her dreams there was always a man — a girl's picture is never complete without a man — a strong, masterful man, whose will should crush down opposition, and whose abilities should make his name—and incidentally her name—famous all over the world. She herself, of course, was always the foremost figure, the handsomest woman, the best-dressed, the most admired; for Ellen Harriott, though only a girl, and a friendless governess at Kuryong, was not inclined to put herself second to anyone. Having learnt from her father's papers that he was of an old family, she considered herself anybody's equal. Her brain held a crazy enough jumble of ideas, no doubt; but given a strong imagination, no experience, and omnivorous reading, a young girl's mind is exactly the place where fantastic ideas will breed and multiply. She went about with Mrs. Gordon to the small festivities of the district, and was welcomed everywhere, and deferred to by the local settlers; she had yet to know what a snub meant; so the world to her seemed a very easy sort of place to get along in. The coming of the heiress was as light over a trackless ocean. Here was someone who had seen, known, and done all the things which she herself wished to see, know, and do; someone who had travelled on the Continent, tobogganed in Switzerland, ridden in Rotten Row, voyaged in private yachts, hunted in the shires; here was the world at last come to her door—the world of which she had read so much and knew so little.

On the second morning after Miss Grant's arrival, that young lady turned up at breakfast in a tailor-made suit with short skirt and heavy boots, and announced her intention of "walking round the estate;" but as Kuryong—though only a small station, as stations go—was, roughly, ten miles square, this project had to be abandoned. Then she asked Hugh if he would have the servants mustered. He told her that the two servants were in the kitchen, but it turned out that she wanted to interview all the station hands, and it had to be explained that the horse-driver was six miles out on the run with his team, drawing in a load of bark to roof the hay shed, and that Harry Warden was down at the drafting yards, putting in a new trough to hold an arsenical solution, through which the sheep had to tramp to cure their feet; and that everybody else was away out on some business or other. But the young lady stuck to her point, and had the groom and the wood-and-water boy paraded, they being the only two available. The groom was an English importation, and earned her approval by standing in a rigid and deferential attitude, and saying "Yes, Miss," and "No, Miss," when spoken to; but the wood-and-water boy stood with his arms akimbo and his mouth open, and when she asked him how he liked being on the station he said, "Oh, it's not too bad," accompanying his remark with a sickly grin that nearly earned him summary dismissal.

The young lady returned to the house in rather a sharp temper, and found Hugh standing by a cart, which had just got back with her shipwrecked luggage.

"Well, Miss Grant," he said, "the things are pretty right. The water went down in an hour or so, and the luggage on the top only got a little wetting — just a wave now and again. How have you been getting on?"

"Not at all well," she laughed. "I don't understand the people here. I will get you to take me round before I do another thing. It is so different from England. Are you sure my clothes are all right?"

"I can't be sure, of course, but you can unpack them as soon as you like."

It was not long before the various boxes were opened. Ellen Harriott was called in to assist, and the two girls had a real good afternoon, looking at and talking over clothes and jewellery. The things had come fairly well out of the coach disaster. When an English firm makes a water-tight cover for a bag or box, it *is* water-tight; even the waters of Kiley's River had swept over the canvas of Miss Grant's luggage in vain. And when the sacred boxes were opened, what a treasure-trove was unveiled!

The noblest study of mankind is man, but the most fascinating study of womankind is another woman's wardrobe, and the Australian girl found something to marvel at in the quality of the visitor's apparel. Dainty shoes, tailor-made jackets, fashionable short riding-habits, mannish-looking riding-boots, silk undergarments, beautiful jewellery, all were taken out of their packages and duly admired. As each successive treasure was produced, Ellen Harriott's eyes grew rounder with astonishment; and when, out of a travelling bag, there appeared a complete dressing-table outfit of silverware — silver-backed hair-brushes, silver manicure set, silver handglass, and so forth — she drew a long breath of wonder and admiration.

It was her first sight of the vanities of the world, the things that she had only dreamed of. The outfit was not anything extraordinary from an English point of view, but to the bush-bred girl it was a revelation.

"What beautiful things!" she said. "Now, when you go visiting to a country-house in England, do you always take things like these, all these riding-boots and things?"

"Oh, yes. You wouldn't ride without them."

"And do you take a maid to look after them?"

"Well, you must have a maid."

"And when you travel on the Continent, do you take a maid?"

"I always took one."

"What is Paris like? Isn't it just a dream? Did you go to the opera?—Have you been on the Riviera?—Oh, do tell me about those places—is it like you read about in books?—all beautiful, well-dressed women and men with nothing to do—and did you go to Monte Carlo?"

This was all poured out in a rush of words; but in Mary's experience the Continent was merely a place where the Continentals got the better of the English, and she said so.

"Travelling is so mixed up with discomfort, that it loses half its plumage," she said. "I'll tell you all I can about Paris some other time. Now you tell me," she went on, folding carefully a silk blouse and putting it in a drawer, "are there any neighbours here? Will anyone come to call?"

"I'm afraid you'll find it very dull here," said Ellen. "There are no neighbours at all except Poss and Binjie, two young fellows on the next station. The people in town are just the publicans and the storekeeper, and all the selectors around us are a very wild lot. Very few strangers come that we can have in the house. They are nearly all cattle and sheep buyers, and they are either too nervous to say a word, or they talk horses. They always come just after mealtime, too, and we have to get everything laid on the table again—sometimes we have ten meals a day in this house. And the swagmen come all day long, and Mrs. Gordon or I have to go and give them something to eat; there's plenty to do, always. So you see, there are plenty of strangers, but no neighbours."

"What about Mr. Blake?" said Miss Grant. "Isn't he a neighbour?"

It would have needed a much quicker eye than Mary's to catch the half-involuntary movement Ellen Harriott made when Blake's name was mentioned. She flashed a look of enquiry at the heiress that seemed to say, "What interest do you take in Mr. Blake? What is he to you?"

Then the long eyelashes shut down over the dark eyes again, and with an air of indifference she said—

"Oh Mr. Blake? Of course I know him. I dance with him sometimes at the show balls, and all that. I have been out for a ride with him, too. I think he's nice, but Hugh and Mrs. Gordon won't ask him here because he belongs to the selectors, and his mother was a Miss Donohoe. He takes up their cases—and wins them, too. But he never comes here. He always stays down at the hotel when he comes out this way."

"I intend to ask him here," said Miss Grant. "He saved my life."

Again the long eyelashes dropped so as to hide the sparkle of the eyes.

"Of course, if you like to ask him—"

"Do you think he'd come?"

"Yes, I'm sure he would. If you like to write and ask him, Peter could ride down to Donohoe's to-day with a note."

From which it would seem that one, at any rate, of the Kuryong household was not wholly indifferent to Mr. Blake.

CHAPTER IX
SOME VISITORS

After breakfast next morning Mary decided to spend the day in the company of the children, who were having holidays.

"Just as well for you to learn the house first," said Hugh, "before you tackle the property. The youngsters know where everything is—within four miles, anyhow."

Two little girls were impressed, and were told to take Miss Grant round and show her the way about the place; and they set off together in the bright morning sunlight, on a trip of exploration.

Now, no true Australian, young or old, ever takes any trouble or undergoes any exertion or goes anywhere without an object in view. So the children considered it the height of stupidity to walk simply for the sake of walking, and kept asking where they were to walk to.

"What shall we see if we go along this road?" asked Miss Grant, pointing with her dainty parasol along the wheel-track that meandered across the open flat and lost itself in the timber.

"Nothing," said both children together.

"Then, what is there up that way?" she asked, waving her hand up towards the foothills and the blue mountains. "There must be some pretty flowers to look at up there?"

"No, there isn't," said the children.

"Well, let us go into the woods and see if we can't find something," she said determinedly; and with her reluctant guides she set off, trudging across the open forest through an interminable vista of gum trees.

After a while one of the girls said, "Hello, there's Poss!"

Miss Grant looked up, and saw through the trees a large and very frightened bay horse, with a white face. On further inspection, a youth of about eighteen or twenty was noticed on the horse's back, but he seemed so much a part of the animal that one might easily overlook him at a first glance. The horse had stopped at the sight of them, and was visibly affected with terror.

They advanced slowly, and the animal began snorting and sidling away among the timber, its rider meanwhile urging it forward. Then Emily cried,

"Hello, Poss!" and the horse gave a snort, wheeled round, jumped a huge fallen tree, and fled through the timber like a wild thing, with its rider still apparently glued to its back. In half a second they were out of sight.

"Who is it? and why does he go away?" asked Miss Grant.

"That's Poss," said Emily carelessly. "He and Binjie live over at Dunderalligo. He often comes here. They and their father live over there That's a colt he's breaking in. He's very nice. So is Binjie."

"Well, here he comes again," said Miss Grant, as the horseman reappeared, riding slowly round them in ever-lessening circles; the colt meanwhile eyeing them with every aspect of intense dislike and hatred, and snorting between whiles like a locomotive.

Emily waited till the rider came fairly close, and said, "Poss, this is Miss Grant."

The rider blushed, and lifted his hand to his hat. Fatal error! For the hundredth-part of a second the horse seemed to cower under him as if about to sink to the ground, then tucked his head in between his front legs, and his tail in between the hind ones, forming himself into a kind of circle, and began a series of gigantic bounds at the rate of about a hundred to the minute; while in the air above him his rider described a catherine wheel before he came to earth, landing on his head at Miss Grant's feet. The horse was soon out of sight, making bounds that would have cleared a house if one had been in the way. The rider got up, pulled his hat from over his eyes, brushed some mud off his clothes, and came up to shake hands as if nothing had happened; his motto apparently being *toujours la politesse*.

"My word, can't he buck, Poss!" said the child. "He chucked you all right, didn't he?"

"He got a mean advantage," said the young fellow, in a slow drawl. "Makes me look a fair chump, doesn't it, getting chucked before a lady? I'll take it out of him when I get on him again. How d' you do?"

"I'm very well, thank you," said Miss Grant. "I hope you are not hurt. What a nasty beast! I wonder you aren't afraid to ride him."

"I ain't afraid of him, the cow! He can't sling me fair work, not the best day ever he saw. He can't buck," he added, in tones of the deepest contempt, "and he won't try when I've got a fair hold of him; only goes at it underhanded. It's up to me to give him a hidin' next time I ride him, I promise you."

"Where will he go to?" said Miss Grant, looking for the vanished steed. "Won't he run away?"

"He can't get out of the paddock," drawled the youth. "Let's go up to the house, and get one of the boys to run him in. He had a go-in this morning with me—the bit came out of his mouth somehow, and he did get to work proper. He went round and round the paddock at home, with me on him, buckin' like a brumby. Binjie had to come out with another horse and run me back into the yard. He's a pretty clever colt, too. The timber is tremendous thick in that paddock, and he never hit me against anything. Binjie reckons any other colt'd have killed me. Come on up to the house, or he'll have my saddle smashed before I get him."

As they hurried home, Miss Grant had a good look at the stranger—a pleasant, brown-skinned brown-handed youth, with the down of a black moustache growing on his upper lip. His frank and open face was easy to read. He looked with boyish admiration at Miss Grant, who immediately stooped to conquer, and began an animated conversation about nothing in particular—a conversation which was broken in upon by one of the girls.

"Where is Binjie?" she asked. "Isn't he coming over?"

"Not he," said the youth, with an air of great certainty. "We're busy over at our place, I tell you. The water is all gone in the nine-mile paddock. Binj an me and Andy Kelly had to muster all the sheep and shift 'em across to the home paddock. Binj is musterin' away there now. I just rode over to see Hugh about some of your sheep that's in the river paddock."

"Won't Binjie be over, then?" persisted Emily.

"No, of course he won't. Don't I tell you he's got three days' work musterin' there? I must be off at daylight to-morrow, home again, or the old man'll know the reason why."

By this time they had reached the homestead, and Poss went off with the children to the stables. Here he secured the "knockabout" horse, always kept saddled and bridled about the station for generally-useful work, and set off at a swinging canter up the paddock after his own steed. Miss Grant went in and found Mrs. Gordon at her jam-making.

"Well, and have you found anything to amuse you?" asked the old lady in her soft, even voice.

"Oh, I've had quite a lot of experiences; and I went for a walk and met Poss. Who is Poss?"

The old lady laughed as she gave the jam a stir. "He's a young Hunter," she said. "Was Binjie there?"

"No; and he isn't coming either; he has work to do. I learnt that much. But who is Poss? and who is Binjie? I'm greatly taken with Poss."

"He's a nice-looking young fellow, isn't he? His father has a small station away among the hills, and Poss and Binjie help him on it. Those are only nick-names, of course. Poss's name is Arthur, and Binjie's is George, I think. They're nice young fellows, but very bushified; they have lived here all their lives. Their father—well, he isn't very steady; and they like to get over here when they can, and each tries to come without the other knowing it. Binjie will be here before long, I expect. They're great admirers of Miss Harriott, both of them, and they come over on all sorts of ridiculous pretexts. Poor fellows, it must be very dull for them over there. Fancy, week after week without seeing anyone but their father, the station-hands, and the sheep! Now that you're here, I expect they'll come more than ever."

As she spoke, the tramp of a horse's hoofs was heard in the yard and, looking out, Miss Grant saw a duplicate of Poss dismounting from a duplicate of Poss's horse. And Mrs. Gordon, looking over her shoulder, said, "Here's Binjie. I thought he'd be here before long."

"Why do they call him Binjie?" asked Miss Grant, watching the new arrival tying up his horse. "What does it mean?"

"It's a blackfellow's word, meaning stomach," said the old lady. "He used to be very fat, and the name stuck to him. Good day, Binjie!"

"Good day, Mrs. Gordon. Hugh at home?"

"No, he won't be back till dark," said the old lady. "Won't you let your horse go?"

"Well, I don't know if I can," replied the new arrival thoughtfully. "I've left Poss at home clearing the sheep out of that big paddock at the Crossing. There's five thousand sheep, and no water there; I'll have to go back and help him. I only came over to tell Hugh there were some of his weaners in the river paddock. I must go straight back, or Poss'll make a row. We've a lot of work to do."

"I think Poss is here," said Mrs. Gordon.

"Poss is here, is he? Well, if that don't beat everything! And when we started to muster that paddock I went to the top, and he went the other way, and he reckoned to be at it all day. He's a nice fellow, he is! I wonder what the old man'll say?"

"Oh, I expect he won't mind very much. This is Mr. George Hunter, Miss Grant."

Binjie extended much the same greeting as Poss had done; and by dinner-time that evening—or, as it is always called in the bush, tea-time—they had all made each other's acquaintance, and both the youths were worshipping at the new shrine.

At tea the talk flowed freely, and the two bush boys, shy at first, began to expand as Mary Grant talked to them. Put a pretty girl and a young and impressionable bushman together, and in the twinkling of an eye you have a Sir Galahad ready to do anything for the service of his lady.

Lightheartedly they consented to stay the night, in the hope of seeing Hugh, to deliver their message about the weaners—they seemed to have satisfactorily arranged the question of mustering. And when Miss Grant said, "Won't your sheep be dying of thirst in that paddock, where there is no water?" both brothers replied, "Oh, we'll be off at crack of dawn in the morning and fix 'em up all right."

"They always say that," said the old lady, "and generally stay three days. I expect they'll make it four, now that you're here."

CHAPTER X
A LAWYER IN THE BUSH

Gavan Blake, attorney and solicitor, sat in his office at Tarrong, opening his morning's letters. The office was in a small weatherboard cottage in the "main street" of Tarrong (at any rate it might fairly claim to be the main street, as it was the only street that had any houses in it). The front room, where he sat, was fitted up with a table and a set of pigeon-holes full of dusty papers, a leather couch, a small fire-proof safe, and a bookcase containing about equal proportions of law-books and novels. A few maps of Tarrong township and neighbouring stations hung on the walls. The wooden partition of the house only ran up to the rafters, and over it could plainly be heard his housekeeper scrubbing his bedroom. Across the little passage was his sitting-room, furnished in the style of most bachelors' rooms, an important item of furniture being a cupboard where whisky was always to be found. At the back of the main cottage were servants' quarters and kitchen. Behind the house, on a spare allotment, were two or three loose-boxes for racehorses, a saddle-room and a groom's room. This was the whole establishment. A woman came in every day to do up his rooms from the hotel, where he had his meals. It was an inexpensive mode of life, but one that conduced to the drinking of a good many whiskies-and-sodas at the hotel with clients and casual callers, and to a good deal of card-playing and late hours. The racehorses, too, like most racehorses, ate up more money than they earned. So that Mr. Gavan Blake, though a clever man, with a good practice, always seemed to find himself hard up.

It was so on this particular morning. Every letter that he opened seemed to have some reference to money. One, from the local storekeeper, was a pretentious account embracing all sorts of items—ammunition, stationery, saddlery and station supplies (the latter being on account of a small station that Blake had taken over for a bad debt, which seemed likely to turn out an equally bad asset). Station supplies, even for bad stations, run into a lot of money, and the store account was approaching a hundred pounds. Then there was a letter from a horse-trainer in Sydney to whom he had sent a racehorse, and though this animal had done such brilliant gallops that the trainer had three times telegraphed him that a race was a certainty—once he went so far as to say that the horse could stop to throw a somersault and still win the race—on each occasion it had always come in among the ruck; and every time forty or fifty pounds of Blake's money had been lost in betting. For Blake was a confirmed gambler, a heavy card-player and backer of horses, and he had the contempt for other people's skill and opinions which seems an inevitable ingredient in the character of brilliant men of a certain type.

He was a man of splendid presence, with strong features and clear blue-grey eyes—the type of face that is seen on the Bench and among the Queen's Counsel in the English Courts. He was quick-witted, eloquent, and logical of mind. Among the Doyles and Donohoes he was little short of a king. Wild, uneducated, and suspicious, they believed in him implicitly. They swore exactly the things that he told them to swear, spoke or were silent according as he ordered, and trusted him with secrets which they would not entrust to their own brothers. In that district he wielded a power greater than the law.

On this particular day, after opening the trainer's letter asking for cheque to pay training expenses (£50), and one from a client, saying "I got your note, and will pay you when I get the wool money," he came upon a letter that startled him. It was written in an old-fashioned, lady's hand, angular and spidery. It ran—

Kuryong Station,
Monday.

Dear Mr. Blake,

Miss Grant tells me that she owes her life to your bravery in saving her from the coach accident. It would give me great pleasure if you would come and stay here next Saturday, as I suppose you will be passing down this way to the Court at Ballarook. With best wishes,

Yours truly,
ANNETTE GORDON.

Blake put the letter down and walked about his office for a while in thought. "Invited to the old station?" he mused. "I must go, of course, Too good a chance to miss."

"Might have written herself!" he muttered, as he turned the letter over to see if by chance Miss Grant had written a line anywhere; then, laying it on one side, he took up carelessly a square business-like envelope, addressed to him in a scrawly, illiterate fist. The letter that he took out of it was a strange jewel to repose in so rude a casket. It also was from Kuryong—from Ellen Harriott, who had taken the precaution of addressing it in a feigned hand so that the postmaster and postmistress at Kiley's Crossing, who handled all station letters, would not know that she was corresponding with Blake. The letter was a great contrast to Mrs. Gordon's. It was a girl's love letter, a gushing, impulsive thing, full of vows and endearments; but the only part of it with which we are concerned ran in this way:—

And so the heiress has arrived at last—and you saved her life! When you swam with her, didn't you feel that you had the weight of a hundred thousand sovereigns on your back? For oh, Gavan dear, she is nice, but she is very stolid! And so you saved her—what luck for you! But you always have luck, don't you? And don't you think that my love is the best bit of luck you have ever had! Everyone says you are making a fortune—hurry up and make it, for I am so anxious to get away out of this place, and we can have our trip round the world together.

And now I am waiting for next Saturday. Fancy having you in the house all day long and in the evening! We must slip away somewhere for just a little while, so that we can have each other all to ourselves. Hugh is still worrying about some sheep that he thinks are stolen. He is always worrying about something or other, and now that she has come I suppose he will be worse than ever. Now goodnight, dearest...

Blake read the letter, and threw it down carelessly on the table; then, leaning back in his chair, cut up a pipeful of tobacco. He thought over his position with Ellen Harriott. There was a secret understanding between them, a sort of informal affair born of moonlight rides and country dances. He had never actually asked her to marry him, but he had kissed her as he had kissed scores of others, and the girl had at once taken it for granted that they were to be engaged. It had not seemed such a bad thing for him at the time. He was fond of her in a ballroom-and-moonlight-ride kind of way, but there it stopped. Still, it was not a bad match for him. The girl was a lady, with friends all over the district. He was rather near the border-line of respectability, and to marry her would have procured him a position that he had little chance of reaching otherwise. He had let things drift on, and the girl, with her fanciful ideas, was, of course, only too ready to fall in with the suggestion of secrecy; it seemed such a precious secret to her. So now he was engaged while still up to his neck in debt; but worse remained behind. In his business he had sums of money for investments and for settlements of cases passing through his hands; and from time to time he had, when hard pushed, used his clients' money to pay his own debts. Beginning with small sums, he had muddled along, meaning to make all straight out of the first big case he had; and each time he had a big case the money seemed to be all spent before he earned it. He was not exactly bankrupt, for he was owed a great deal of money, enough perhaps to put him straight if he could get it in; but the mountain folk expected long credit and large reductions, and it was pretty certain that he would never get even half of what he was owed. Therefore, he went about his business with a sort of sword of Damocles hanging over his head—and now the heiress had come, and he had saved her life!

His musings were cut short by a tap at the door; a long, gawky youth, with a budding moustache, entered and slouched over to a chair. He was young Isaacstein, son of the Tarrong storekeeper, a would-be sportsman, would-be gambler, would-be lady-killer, would-be everything, who only succeeded in making himself a cheap bar-room loafer; but he was quite satisfied that he was the right thing.

"What's doing, Gav?" he said. "Who's the letter from?"

"Oh, business—business" said Gavan Blake.

"What's doing with you?"

"Doing! By Gad, I'm broke. The old man won't give me a copper. What about Saturday? Are you going to the Court at Ballarook?"

"Yes. I've got a couple of cases there. And I've just got a letter from Mrs. Gordon, asking me to stay the night at Kuryong."

"Ho! My oath! Stop at Kuryong, eh? That's cause you saved the heiress? Well, go in and win. You won't know us when you marry the owner of Kuryong. What's she like, Gav? Pretty girl, ain't she? Has she any sense?"

"Much as you have," growled Blake.

"Oh, don't get nasty. Only I thought you were a bit shook on the governess there—what about that darnce at the Show ball, eh? I say, you couldn't lend us a tenner till Saturday?"

"No, I could not—" And this was the literal truth, for Gavan Blake had run himself right out of money, and was living on credit—not an enviable position at any time, and one doubly insupportable to a man of his temperament. And again his thoughts went back to the girl he had saved, and he pondered how different things might have been—might, perhaps, still be.

CHAPTER XI
A WALK IN THE MOONLIGHT

The Court at Ballarook was over, and Gavan Blake turned his horses' heads in a direction he had never taken before—along the road to Kuryong. As he drove along, his thoughts were anything but pleasant. Behind him always stalked the grim spectre of detection and arrest; and, even should a lucky windfall help to pay his debts, he could not save the money either to buy a practice in Sydney or to maintain himself while he was building one up. He thought of the pitiful smallness of his chances at Tarrong, and then of Ellen Harriott. What should he do about her? Well, sufficient unto the day was the evil thereof. He would play for his own hand throughout. With which reflection he drove into the Kuryong yard.

When he drove up, the family had gathered round the fire in the quaint, old-fashioned, low-ceiled sitting-room; for the evenings were still chilly. The children were gravely and quietly sharpening terrific-looking knives on small stones; the old lady had some needlework; while Mary and Ellen and Poss and Binjie talked about horses, that being practically the only subject open to the two boys.

After a time Mrs. Gordon said, "Won't you sing something?" and Mary sat down to the piano and sang to them. Such singing no one there had ever heard before. Her deep contralto voice was powerful, flexible, and obviously well-trained; besides which she had the great natural gift of putting "feeling" into her singing. The children sat spellbound. The station-hands and house-servants, who had been playing the concertina and yarning on the wood-heap at the back of the kitchen, stole down to the corner of the house to listen; in the stillness that wonderful voice floated out into the night. So it chanced that Gavan Blake, arriving, heard the singing, stole softly to the door, and looked in, listening for a while, before anyone saw him.

The picture he saw was for ever photographed on his mind. He saw the quiet comfort and luxury—for after Tarrong it was luxury to him—of the station drawing-room; caught the scent of the flowers and the glorious tones of that beautiful voice; and, as he watched the sweet face of the singer, and listened to the words of the song, a sudden fierce determination rose in his mind. He would devote all his energies to winning Mary Grant for his wife; combative and self-confident as he was by nature, he felt no dismay at the difficulties in his way. He had been on a borderline long enough. Here was his chance to rise at a bound, and he determined to succeed if success were humanly possible.

As the song came to an end, he walked into the drawing-room and shook hands all round, Mary being particularly warm in her welcome.

"You are very late," said the old lady. "Was there much of a Court at Ballarook?"

"Only the usual troubles. You know what those courts are. By the way, Miss Grant, I came over the famous crossing-place where we got turned out, and nearly had another swim for it. Martin Donohoe and his wife haven't yet finished talking about how wet you looked."

"I'm sure I haven't finished thinking about it. I don't suppose you had to swim with anyone on your back this time?"

"No such luck, I'm sorry to say."

"It was very lucky, indeed—that you were there," put in Miss Harriott. "You are really quite the district hero, Mr. Blake. *You* will have to save somebody next, Hugh."

"My word," said Poss, "I've seen Hugh swim in to fetch a sheep, let alone a lady. You remember, Hugh, the time those old ewes got swept down and one of 'em was caught on the head of a tree, and you went in—"

"Oh, never mind about that," said Hugh. "Did Pat Donohoe lose anything out of the coach?"

"Only a side of bacon and a bottle of whisky. The whisky was for old Ned the 'possum trapper, and they say that Ned walked fourteen miles down the river in hopes that it might have come ashore. Ned reckons he has never done any tracking, but if he could track anything it would be whisky."

"What about going out after 'possums down the garden?" said Binjie. "Now, you youngsters, where are your 'possum dogs? I think they ought to get some in the garden."

Everyone seemed to welcome the idea. There had been a sort of stiffness in the talk, and Gavan Blake felt that a walk in the moonlight might give him a chance to make himself a little more at home with Mary Grant, while Ellen Harriott had her own reasons for wanting to get him outside. With laughter and haste they all put on hats and coats, for it had turned bitterly cold; then with ear-piercing whistles the children summoned their 'possuming dogs, who were dreaming happy hours away in all sorts of odd nooks, in chimney-corners, under the table in the kitchen, under the bunks in the men's hut, anywhere warm and undisturbed. But at the whistles each dog dashed out from his nook, tearing over everything in front of him in his haste not to be left behind; and in three seconds half a dozen of them were whining and jumping round the children, waiting for orders which way to go.

A majestic wave of the hand, and the order "Go and find him!" from the eldest of the children, sent a hurricane of dogs yapping with excitement off to the creek, and the hunters followed at a brisk run. Gavan Blake and Mary Grant trotted along together in the bright moonlight. Just in front were Ellen and Hugh, he laughing at the excitement of the dogs and children, she looking over her shoulder and hoping to hear what Blake was saying to the heiress. As a matter of fact, he was making the most of his chances, and before long they were getting on capitally. Mary found herself laying aside her slow English way, and laughing and joking with the rest. There is something intoxicating in moonlight at any time; and what with the moon and the climate, and the breeze whistling through the gum-boughs, it was no wonder that even the staidly-reared English girl felt a thrill of excitement, a stirring of the primeval instincts that civilization and cultivation had not quite been able to choke.

"When you go back to England, Miss Grant," said Blake, "you will be able to tell them that you have hunted 'possums, anyhow. That will sound like the real bush, won't it?"

"Yes. And I can say I have been upset in a river and nearly drowned, too. I'm becoming quite an experienced person. But what makes you think I shall go back to England?"

"I thought you would be sure to go back."

"Oh, no. We have no friends in England at all. My mother's people are nearly all living in India, and father wouldn't live in England. He hates it."

"And do you like Australia?"

"I've only seen about a week of it. Do you know, it seems to me a more serious life than in England. Look at Mrs. Gordon, what a lot of people she has dependent on her. The station-hands and their wives, all come to her. In England she might visit them and give them tracts and blankets, but here what they want is advice and help in all sorts of things. You know what I mean?"

"Yes. She is a fine old lady, isn't she? A real character. You will be sure to like her."

"Yes. I think I shall be very happy here. Father is anxious I should like this place, as he may come up here to live, and I'm sure I shall like it. You see, there is work to do here. Miss Harriott and Mrs. Gordon are at work from daylight till dark; what with the children, the house, the store and visitors, there really isn't time to feel lonely. Don't you think people are much happier when they have a lot to do? Do you live—"

"I live in two rooms and get my meals at an hotel, Miss Grant. I have never had any home life. I never knew what it meant till now."

"You must come out again when you are down this way. The—what's that?"

A dog barked furiously in the distance, and the others rushed to join him from all directions, yelping and squealing with excitement. The whole party set off at a run, amid cheers and laughter.

"What is it, what is it?" said Mary.

"One of the dogs has found a 'possum up a tree, and the children will try to get him down. Come on! Mind where you go. The black shadows are very hard to judge, and sometimes a log or a bush is hidden in them. There goes Poss over a log," he added, in explanation of a terrific crash and a shout of laughter from the others. "What is it, Emily?" he asked as one of the children ran past.

"It's Thomas Carlyle has found one," she said, "and he never barks when the 'possums are up big trees. He knows we can't get them then, so he only looks in the saplings. The other dogs find them in the big trees, but that's no good."

A sharp run brought the party to the foot of a small tree, surrounded by a circle of dogs, all sitting on their tails and staring with whimpers of anxiety up to the topmost branches, where a small furry animal was perched. Mary Grant, under Blake's directions, got the animal silhouetted against the moon, and saw clearly enough the sharp nose, round ears, plump body, and prehensile tail of the unfortunate creature who, as Poss said, looked as if he were wishing for a pair of wings.

Blake turned to Mary. "Do you want to stop and see it killed?" he said. "It's rather a murderous business. The 'possum has no chance. One of the boys will go up the tree and shake the branch till the 'possum falls off, and when it falls the dogs will kill it."

"No, I don't think I would like to see it. I have seen so many things killed since I came here. Let us walk back towards the house."

"I'll tell Gordon. Gordon," he said, "Miss Grant doesn't care to see the massacre. We will walk back towards the house."

Ellen Harriott made a sudden step forward. "I will go back too," she said.

"Why, Miss Harriott!" said Poss in astonishment, "You've seen lots of 'em killed. Native cats, too. Watch me knock him out of that with a stick."

"No, no, I'll go back, too. I don't feel like killing anything to-night. You come back too, Hugh."

So the four walked back together, and as Blake had monopolised Mary on the way out, she now put herself beside Hugh, and the others walked behind. Hugh and Mary soon began to talk, but the other pair walked in silence for a while. Then Ellen Harriott said in a low voice, "Go a little slower, Gavan. Let them get away." As they passed under the dense shadows of a huge wild-apple tree, Ellen stopped and, turning to Blake, held up her face to be kissed.

"Gavan, Gavan!" she said. "I was wondering when I would ever get a chance to speak to you. To think of you being here in the same house with me! It's too wonderful, isn't it?"

Gavan Blake kissed her. It was almost an effort to him at first, as his mind and heart were on fire with the thoughts of the other girl.

"My darling, my darling!" she said. "All the while you were walking with that girl, I knew you were dying to come and kiss me!" For such is the faith of women.

They stopped for a little while, and then moved on after the others, pausing now and again in the shadows. The girl poured out all her artless tale—how she had been awake night after night, waiting for the day he should come. Then she told him how the heiress had praised his pluck and strength. "And oh! Gavan, I was so proud, I could have hugged her!"

Thus she rattled on, while he, because it was his nature found it no trouble to reply in kind, with a good imitation of sincerity. On such a night, with such a girl clinging to him, it would have been a very poor specimen of a man who could not have trumped up a sort of enthusiasm. But in his heart he was cursing his luck that just as chance had thrown the heiress in his way, and put her under an obligation to him, he was held to his old bargain—the bargain that he had made for position's sake, and which he would now have liked to break for the same reason.

It would be wearisome to record their talk, all the way up to the house. The girl—impetuous, hot-blooded, excitable—poured out her love-talk like a bird singing. Happiness complete was hers for the time; but Gavan's heart was not in the wooing, and he listened and was silent.

Hugh and Mary, walking on ahead, knew nothing of the love scenes just behind them. They talked of many things, of the moonlight and the river and the scent of the flowers, but all the time Hugh felt diffident and tongue-tied. He had not the glib tongue of Gavan Blake, and he felt little at ease talking common-places. Mary Grant thought he must be worried over something, and, with her usual directness, went to the point.

"You are worrying over something," she said. "What is it?"

"Oh, no; nothing."

"It is not because I asked Mr. Blake here, is it?"

"Oh no! Goodness, no! Why, he is fifty times better than most of the people that come here. It just happens we had never asked him before. I think he is a very nice fellow."

"I'm glad of that. I have asked him to come out again. He seems to know Miss Harriott quite well, though he doesn't know your mother."

"Yes, he met Miss Harriott at some of the race-balls, I think. She is a queer girl, full of fancies."

"She seems a very quiet sort of girl to me," said Miss Grant. But if she could have known what was going on about two hundred yards behind her, she might have altered her opinion.

CHAPTER XII
MR. BLAKE BREAKS HIS ENGAGEMENT

On Monday, Hugh, Poss, and Binjie had to go out to an outlying paddock to draft a lot of station-sheep from a mob of travelling-sheep. As this meant a long, hard job, the three breakfasted by candlelight—a good old fashion, this, but rather forgotten lately—and Blake also turned out for early breakfast, as he wanted to get his drive to Tarrong over while the weather was cool. Of the women-folk, Ellen alone was up, boiling eggs, and making tea on a spirit-lamp; laughing and chattering meanwhile, and keeping them all amused; while outside in the frosty dawn, the stable boy shivered as he tightened the girths round the ribs of three very touchy horses. Poss and Binjie were each riding a station horse to "take the flashness out of him," and Binjie's horse tried to buck him off, but might as well have tried to shed his own skin; so he bolted instead, and disappeared with a snort and a rattle of hoofs over the hill. The others followed, with their horses very much inclined to go through the same performance.

After they had gone, Ellen Harriott and Blake were left alone in the breakfast-room. Outside, the heedless horse-boy was harnessing Blake's ponies; but inside no one but themselves was awake, and as he finished his breakfast, Ellen stepped up to the table and blew out the two candles, leaving the room in semi-darkness. She caught his hand, and he drew her to him. It was what she had been waiting for all night. She had pictured a parting, which was to be such sweet sorrow. Blake had also pictured it to himself, but in quite a different way.

He was determined to make an end of his engagement (or entanglement, whichever it could be called), and yet when the chance came he almost put it off; but the thought of what exposure and disgrace would mean, if his affairs were investigated, drove him on.

He stroked her hair for a while in silence, and then, with a laugh, said, "We'll have to give up this sort of thing, you know; it'll be getting you talked about, and that'll never do."

She hardly knew what he meant. Having lived so long in a fool's paradise, she could not realise that her world was coming down about her ears.

"We'll have to be proper in future," he said. "I've had the most fiendish run of bad luck lately, and it's just as well there never was any engagement between us. It would have had to come to nothing."

She drew back, and looked at him with frightened eyes. He had great power over her—this big, masterful man, whom she had looked upon as her lover; and she could not believe that a little trouble about money could really make any difference to him. She believed him able to overcome any such difficulty as that of earning a living for her and himself.

"But, Gavan," she said, "what have I done?"

"Done, little girl? you've done nothing. It's all my fault. I've lost heart over things lately, and it will only harm you if we keep up this pretence of being engaged. Nothing can come of it."

"Why not? Why can't we wait?"

"Wait! To be stuck in Tarrong all my life among these people, and up to my neck in debt! No, little woman, as soon as ever I can get things squared up, I'm off out of this, and I dare say we'll never see each other again. I've made a mess of things here, and I'm off somewhere else."

It seemed almost incredible to her that a man could so throw up the fight; and then a thought flashed into her mind.

"It is not because Miss Grant has come that you do this?"

He laughed with a well-simulated indifference.

"Miss Grant!" he said, "I have only seen her twice—that day on the coach and last night."

She seemed to study the question, still holding his hands, and looking up into his face. The light in the room was stronger, and there were sounds as if some of the household were stirring.

"So we must say 'Good-bye!'" she said, "just because you are short of money. Gavan, I would have thought more of you, had you told me you were tired of me and were going in for the other girl. I think I could have respected you at any rate; but to sneak out on the story of not being able to afford it—"

His face darkened, and he began to speak, but she stopped him, and went on in a passionless sort of voice. "Some one is coming," she said, "and we must say good-bye; and since you wish it, it *is* Good-bye.' But I'm not a child, to change my fancies in a day, so I won't promise to forget. And I think you have treated me very badly, so neither will I promise to forgive. I had set my heart on you, Gavan. You seemed to me—but there, it's no use talking. I suppose I *should* be meek and mild, and—"

"But, Ellen—"

"No, don't interrupt me. It is the last talk together we shall have. I suppose I can go governessing, or nursing, to the end of the chapter. It seems a dreary outlook, doesn't it? Now go, and remember that I do not forgive easily. I had built such castles, Gavan, and now—" She slipped quietly from the room, and was gone.

Gavan Blake drove home, feeling a trifle uneasy. He had expected some sort of outburst, but the curious way in which she had taken it rather nonplussed him.

"She won't stick a knife in herself, I suppose," he mused. "Just like her to do something unusual. Anyway, she has too much pride to talk about it—and the affair had to come to an end sooner or later."

And feeling that if not "on with the new love," he was, at any rate, satisfactorily "off with the old," Blake drove his spanking ponies off to Tarrong, while Ellen Harriott went about her household work with a face as inscrutable and calm as though no stone had ruffled the mill-pond of her existence.

CHAPTER XIII
THE RIVALS

For the next couple of weeks, affairs at Kuryong flowed on in usual station style. A saddle-horse was brought in for Miss Grant, and out of her numerous boxes that young lady produced a Bond Street outfit that fairly silenced criticism. She rode well too, having been taught in England, and she, Poss, Binjie and Hugh had some great scampers after kangaroos, half-wild horses, or anything else that would get up and run in front of them. She was always so fresh, cheerful, and ready for any excitement that the two boys became infatuated in four days, and had to be hunted home on the fifth, or they would have both proposed. Some days she spent at the homestead housekeeping, cooking, and giving out rations to swagmen—the wild, half-crazed travellers who came in at sundown for the dole of flour, tea and sugar, which was theirs by bush custom. Some days she spent with the children, and with them learnt a lot of bush life. It being holiday-time, they practically ran wild all over the place, spending whole days in long tramps to remote parts in pursuit of game. They had no "play," as that term is known to English children. They didn't play at being hunters. They were hunters in real earnest, and their habits and customs had come to resemble very closely those of savage tribes that live by the chase.

With them Mary had numberless new experiences. She got accustomed to seeing the boys climb big trees by cutting steps in the bark with a tomahawk, going out on the most giddy heights after birds' nests, or dragging the opossum from his sleeping-place in a hollow limb. She learned to hold a frenzied fox-terrier at the mouth of a hollow log, ready to pounce on the kangaroo-rat which had taken refuge there, and which flashed out as if shot from a catapult on being poked from the other end with a long stick. She learned to mark the hiding-place of the young wild-ducks that scuttled and dived, and hid themselves with such super-natural cunning in the reedy pools. She saw the native companions, those great, solemn, grey birds, go through their fantastic and intricate dances, forming squares, pirouetting, advancing, and retreating with the solemnity of professional dancing-masters. She lay on the river-bank with the children, gun in hand, breathless with excitement, waiting for the rising of the duck-billed platypus—that quaint combination of fish, flesh and fowl—as he dived in the quiet waters, a train of small bubbles marking his track. She fished in deep pools for the great, sleepy, hundred-pound cod-fish that sucked down bait and hook, *holus-bolus*, and then were hauled in with hardly any resistance, and lived for days contentedly, tethered to the bank by a line through their gills.

In these amusements time passed pleasantly enough, and by the time school-work was resumed Mary Grant had become one of the family.

Of Hugh she at first saw little. His work took him out on the run all day long, looking after sheep in the paddocks, or perhaps toiling day after day in the great, dusty drafting-yards. In the cool of the afternoon the two girls would often canter over the four miles or so of timbered country to the yards, and wait till Hugh had finished his day's work. As a rule, Poss or Binjie, perhaps both, were in attendance to escort Miss Harriott, with the result that Hugh and Mary found themselves paired off to ride home together. Before long he found himself looking forward to these rides with more anxiety than he cared to acknowledge, and in a very short time he was head over ears in love with her.

Any man, being much alone with any woman in a country house, will fall in love with her; but a man such as Hugh Gordon, ardent, imaginative, and very young, meeting every day a woman as beautiful as Mary Grant, was bound to fall a victim. He soon became her absolute worshipper. All day long, in the lonely rides through the bush, in the hot and dusty hours at the sheep-yards, through the pleasant, lazy canter home in the cool of the evening, his fancies were full of her—her beauty and her charm. It was happiness enough for him to be near her, to feel the soft touch of her hand, to catch the faint scent that seemed to linger in her hair. After the day's work they would stroll together about the wonderful old garden, and watch the sunlight die away on the western hills, and the long strings of wild fowl hurrying down the river to their nightly haunts. Sometimes he would manage to get home for lunch, and afterwards, on the pretext of showing her the run, would saddle a horse for her, and off they would go for a long ride through the mountains. Or there were sheep to inspect, or fences to look at—an excuse for an excursion was never lacking.

For the present he made no sign; he was quite contented to act as confidant and adviser, and many a long talk they had together over the various troubles that beset the manager of a station.

It would hardly be supposed that a girl could give much advice on such matters, and at first her total ignorance of the various difficulties amused him; but when she came to understand them better, her cool common-sense compelled his admiration. His temperament was nervous and excitable, and he let things fret him. She took everything in a cheery spirit, and laughed him out of his worries. One would not expect to find many troubles in rearing sheep and selling their wool; but the management of any big station is a heavy task, and Kuryong would have driven Job mad.

The sheep themselves, to begin with, seem always in league against their owners. Merinos, though apparently estimable animals, are in reality dangerous monomaniacs, whose sole desire is to ruin the man that owns them. Their object is to die, and to do so with as much trouble to their owners as they possibly can. They die in the droughts when the grass, roasted to a dull white by the sun, comes out by the roots and blows about the bare paddocks; they die in the wet, when the long grass in the sodden gullies breeds "fluke" and "bottle" and all sorts of hideous complaints. They get burnt in bush fires from sheer malice, refusing to run in any given direction, but charging round and round in a ring till they are calcined. They get drowned by refusing to leave flooded country, though hunted with frenzied earnestness.

It was not the sheep so much as the neighbours whose depredations were drawing lines on Hugh Gordon's face. "I wouldn't care," he confided to Miss Grant, "if they only took a beast or two. But the sheep are going by hundreds. We mustered five hundred short in one paddock this month. And there isn't a Doyle or a Donohoe cow but has three calves at least, and two of each three belong to us."

He dared not prosecute them. No local jury would convict in face of the hostility that would be aroused. They had made "alibis" a special study; the very judges were staggered by the calmness and plausibility with which they got themselves out of difficulties.

A big station with a lot of hostile neighbours is like a whale with the killers round it; it is open to attack on all sides, and cannot retaliate. A match dropped carelessly in a patch of grass sets miles of country in a blaze. Hugh, as he missed the stock, and saw fences cut and grass burnt, could only grind his teeth and hope that a lucky chance would put some of the enemy in his power. To Mary it seemed incredible that in the nineteenth century people should be able to steal sheep without suffering for it; and Hugh soon saw that she was a true daughter of William Grant, as far as fighting was concerned. She listened with set teeth to all stories of depredation and trespass, and they talked over many a plan together. But though they became quite friendly their intimacy seemed to make no progress. To her he was rather the employee than the friend. In fact he did not get on half so far as did Gavan Blake, who came up to Kuryong occasionally, and made himself so agreeable that already his name was being coupled with that of the heiress. Ellen Harriott always spoke to Blake when he came to the station, and gave no sign of jealousy at his attentions to Mary Grant; but she was waiting and watching, as one who has been a nurse learns to do. And things were in this state when an unexpected event put an altogether different complexion on affairs.

CHAPTER XIV
RED MICK AND HIS SHEEP DOGS

When Hugh came home one day with his face, as usual, full of trouble, Mary began to laugh him out of it.

"Well, Mr. Hugh, which is it to-day—the Doyles or the Donohoes? Have they been stealing sheep or breaking gates?"

"Oh, it's all very well for you to laugh," he said; "you don't understand. Some of that gang up the river went into the stud paddock yesterday to cut down a tree for a bee's nest, and left the tree burning; might have set the whole run—forty thousand acres of dry grass—in a blaze. Then they drove their dray against the gate, knocking it sideways, and a lot of the stud sheep got out into the other paddock, and I'll have to be off at day-break to-morrow to get 'em back."

"Why don't you summon the wretches, and have them put in gaol, or go and break their gates, and cut down their trees?" she said, with a cheerful ignorance of details.

"I daren't—simply daren't. If I summoned one of them, I'd never have dry grass but there'd be fires. I'd never have fat sheep but there'd be dogs among 'em. *They* ride all over the run; but if a bird belonging to the station flew over one of their selections they'd summon me for trespass. There's no end to the injury a spiteful neighbour can do you in this sort of country. And your father would blame me."

"Why?"

"Oh, it's part of the management of a station to get on with your neighbours. Never quarrel if you can help it. But since shearing troubles started we have no friends at all."

"Well," she said, "I should like to have a look at those desperate neighbours I hear so much about. Red Mick Donohoe rode past the other day on such a beautiful horse, and he opened the gate for us, and asked if he might come down to hear me sing. Think of that, now."

"Very well," he said. "We'll go for a ride up that way to-morrow afternoon. We might find Red Mick killing some of our sheep, and you can go into the box as the lady detective. If you'll only sing him into gaol, the station will pay you at the same rate as Patti gets!"

Next afternoon they cantered away up the river towards the mountains. Poss and Binjie had long ago laid their dearest possessions at her feet, begging her to ride them—horses so precious that it had hitherto been deemed sacrilege to put a side-saddle on them. She had the divine gift of "hands," and all manner of excitable, pulling horses went quietly and smoothly under her management. Her English training had taught her to ride over jumps, and she was very anxious to have a try at post-and-rail fences.

After much pressing, Hugh had this day allowed her to try Obadiah, Binjie's celebrated show jumper, an animal that could be trusted to jump anything he could see over; so during their ride to the habitat of the Donohoes they left the regular track, and followed one of the fences for a mile or two, looking for a suitable place to try the horse. No good place offered itself, as the timber was thick, and the country so rugged that she would have had to ride at a stiff post-and-rail either up or down a steep slope. Loitering along, far off the track, they crossed a little ridge where stringybark trees, with an undergrowth of bushes and saplings, formed a regular thicket.

Suddenly Hugh gave a whistle of surprise, and jumped from his horse.

"Hold this horse a minute, please," he said. "There has been a mob of sheep driven here."

"Whereabouts?" said she, staring round her.

"All about here," he said, pointing to the ground. "Don't you see the tracks? Hundreds of 'em. But I can't see what they were up to. There's no place they could get 'em out without cutting the wires, and the fence is sound enough. Good heavens, I see it now! Well, that's smart he continued, leaning against a post and giving it a shake.

"What have they done I don't understand. How have they got the sheep through without breaking the fence?"

"They've dug up four or five posts," he said, kicking over some red earth with his foot, "laid that piece of fence flat on the ground, driven the sheep over it, and then put the fence up again. No wonder we are missing sheep! Two or three hundred have gone out here! Here's a chance at last—the chance I've been waiting for all these years! What a lucky thing we came here! And now, Miss Grant," he said, remounting, "we won't have any jumping to-day. I'll have to follow these tracks till I come on the sheep somewhere, if it's in Red Mick Donohoe's own yard. Do you think you can find your way back to the homestead?"

"What for?"

"To tell them to send Poss and Binjie after me. I don't expect they've gone home yet. I want a witness with me when I catch Red Mick with these sheep, or else fifty of his clan will swear that he has been in bed for six weeks, or something like that."

"Then," she said firmly, gathering up the reins in her daintily gloved hands as she spoke, "I'm going with you. I'm just as good a witness as Poss or Binjie."

"No, no, no," said Hugh, "that won't do. There may be a row. It's a rough sort of place, and a rough lot of people. Now look here, Miss Grant, oblige me and go home. The horse will take you straight back."

Her eyes glowed with excitement. "Please let me come," she said. "You don't know how much I want to come. I'll do whatever you tell me!"

He argued and expostulated and entreated. He knew well enough there was a good deal of risk in the matter, and he tried hard to make her go back. But she was determined to go with him, and the argument ended in the only possible manner—she went. She promised to do exactly what she was told, to keep out of the way if so ordered, and, above all, not to speak except when spoken to.

So off they went through the scrub on the track of the sheep, plain as print to the young bushman, though invisible to his companion. They rode at a walk for the most part, for fear of being heard. Now and again, when they could see for a good distance ahead, they let the horses canter; Hugh riding in front, she, like a damosel of old, in assumed submission a few lengths behind, and thoroughly enjoying the adventure.

Of course she could not keep silence long, and after a while she drew alongside, and whispered, "Do you think we shall catch them?"

"I hope so. But it's a very curious thing; there has been a dog after these sheep—see, there's his track," pointing to foot-prints plainly marked in wet sand—"but no track of man or horse to be seen. By Jove, look there!"

They had come to the crest of a small hill, and were looking down a long valley. To right and left of them towered the blue, rugged peaks; straight in front the valley opened out, and they got a fairly clear view for a mile or more. About half a mile ahead, travelling in a compact mass down the valley, was a mob of some two or three hundred sheep. At their heels trotted two sheep-dogs of the small wiry breed common in the mountains. Hugh looked about to see who was in charge of them; but no one was visible. The dogs were taking the sheep along without word or sign from anyone, hurrying them at a good sharp pace, each keeping on his own flank of the mob, or occasionally dropping behind to hurry up the laggards.

It was a marvellous exhibition of sagacity. They came to a place where it was necessary to turn sharply to the right to cross a small creek; one of the dogs shot forward, and sent the leading sheep scurrying down the bank, while the other fell back a few yards and prevented the mob turning back. After a moment's hesitation the sheep plunged into the shallow water, splashed across the creek, and set off again in their compact march down the valley, urged and directed by their silent custodians—who paused to lap a few mouthfuls of water, and then hurried on with an air of importance.

"Look at that," said Hugh, in open admiration. "Isn't that wonderful? Those are Red Mick's dogs. I knew they were good dogs, but this is simply marvellous, isn't it? What are we to do now? If I take the sheep from them they'll run home, and I can't prosecute Red Mick because they picked up a mob of sheep."

"Oh, but he must be near them somewhere," said Mary, to whom the whole affair appeared uncanny. "They wouldn't drive sheep by themselves, surely?"

"Oh, of course, he started them. Once he got the sheep out of the paddock, he started the dogs for home, and rode off. You see his plan. If anyone finds the dogs with them, of course he had nothing to do with it. Sheep-dogs will often go into a paddock, and bring a mob of sheep up to the yard on their own account. It's an instinct with them. Look at those two now, forcing the sheep over that bad crossing. Isn't it wonderful?"

"Well," she said, triumphantly, "what about the fence? They couldn't dig up that."

"Oh, Red Mick did; but who's to prove it? He'll swear he never was near the fence, and that his dogs picked up these sheep and brought them home on their own account. The jury would find that I dug up my own fence, and they'd acquit Red Mick, and give him a testimonial. No, I'll tell you what we'll do. We'll cut across the range, and sneak up as near Red Mick's as we can. Then we'll hide and watch his house; and when the dogs come up, if he takes the sheep from them, or starts to drive them anywhere, we've got him. Once he takes charge of those sheep he's done. Of course there may be a bit of trouble when we spring up and accuse him. Are you afraid?"

"No," she replied. "I'm not afraid—with you. I like it. Come on."

No sooner said than done. They set their horses in motion, and went at a steady trot for a mile or so, crossing the valley at right angles, over a sharp rise and down a small hill, till Hugh again pulled up.

"There's Red Mick's homestead," he said, pointing to a speck far away down a gully. "The sheep will come up the creek, because it is the smoothest track. Now, we must tie our horses up here, sneak down the creek bed, and get as near the house as we can."

They tied their horses up in a clump of trees, and made the rest of the journey on foot, hurrying silently for half a mile down the bed of the creek, hidden by its steep banks. Here and there, to escape observation, they had to walk in the water, and Hugh, looking round, saw his companion wading after him, with face firm-set and eyes ablaze. It was a man-hunt, the most exciting of all hunting.

He laughed silently at the girl's flushed and excited face. As he reached out to help her over some fallen timber, she took his hand with a firm grip that set his nerves tingling. They pushed on until almost abreast of Red Mick's dwelling; then Hugh, standing on a projecting stump, peered over the high bank to see how the land lay, while his companion sat down and watched his movements with wide open eyes.

He saw the cottage drowsing in the bright afternoon sunlight. It was a picturesque little building, made of heavy red-gum slabs, with a bark roof; the windows were merely square holes cut in the slabs, fitted with heavy wooden covers that now hung open, giving a view of the interior. In one room could be seen a rough dresser covered with plates and dishes, and a saddle hung from a tie-beam; in the other there was a rough plank bed with blue blankets. The door was shut, and there was no sign of life about the place. There was no garden in front of the house, merely the bare earth and a dust-heap where ashes were thrown out, on which a few hens were enjoying the afternoon sun and fluffing the dust over themselves.

At the back was a fair-sized garden, with fine, healthy-looking trees; and about a quarter of a mile away was the straggling collection of bark-roofed sheds and corkscrew-looking fences that served Red Mick as shearing-sheds for his sheep, and drafting and branding-yards for his cattle and horses. After a hurried survey Hugh dropped lightly down into shelter, and whispered, "There's no one moving at all. There's a newly-fallen tree about a hundred yards down the creek; we'll get among its branches and watch."

They crept along the creek until opposite the fallen tree; there Hugh scaled the bank and pulled Mary up after him. Silent as shadows, they stole through a little patch of young timber, and ensconced themselves among the fragrant branches. The grass was long where the tree had fallen, and this, with the green boughs, made a splendid couch and hiding-place.

They settled close together and peered out like squirrels, first up at the house, then down the valley for the arrival of the sheep. Both were shaking with excitement—she at the unwonted sensation of attacking a criminal in his lair, and he with anxiety lest some unlucky chance should bring his plan to nought, and make him a failure in the eyes of the woman he loved.

"There is no one about," he whispered. "I expect Red Mick has told the family to keep indoors, so that they can swear they saw nothing. You aren't afraid, are you?"

She pressed his arm in answer, gave a low laugh, and pointed down the flat. There, far away among the trees, they saw the white phalanx of the approaching sheep, and the little lean dogs hunting them straight towards the house.

Still no sign from Red Mick. No one stirred about the place; the fowls still fluttered in the dust, and a dissipated looking pet cockatoo, perched on the wood-heap repeated several times in a drowsy tone, "Good-bye, Cockie! Good-bye, Cockie!" Then the door opened, and Red Mick stepped out.

He was the acknowledged leader of the Doyle-Donohoe faction in all matters of cunning, and in all raids on other folks' stock; and not only did he plan the raids, but took a leading part in executing them. He was the finest and most fearless bush rider in the district, and could track like a black fellow. If he left a strange camp at sundown, and rode about the bush all night, he could at any time go back straight across country to his starting point, or to any place he had visited during his wanderings. Such bushmanship is a gift, and not to be learnt. If once he saw a horse, he would know it again for the rest of his life—fat or lean, sick or well. Which is also a gift.

In appearance he was a tall, lanky, large-handed, slab-sided cornstalk, about thirty-five years of age, with a huge red beard that nearly covered his face, and a brick-dust complexion variegated with large freckles. His legs were long and straight; he wore tight-fitting white moleskin trousers, a coloured Crimean shirt, and a battered felt hat.

Miss Grant felt almost sorry for this big, simple-looking bushman, who came strolling past their hiding-place, his eyes fixed on the sheep, and his hands mechanically occupied in cutting up tobacco. Behind him gambolled a half-grown collie pup, evidently a relative of the dogs in charge of the sheep.

They brought the sheep up to a little corner of land formed by a sharp bend of the creek, then stopped, squatting on their haunches as sentinels, and the sheep, fatigued with their long, fast run, settled in under the trees to get out of the sun. Behind the sheep, Hugh caught a glimpse of two horsemen coming slowly up the road towards the house.

"Look! Here's Mick's nephews," he whispered, "come to take the sheep away. By George, we'll bag the whole lot! Sit quiet: don't make a sound."

The crisis approached. Miss Grant, with strained attention, saw Red Mick strike a match, and light his pipe. Strolling on towards the sheep, he passed about thirty yards from where they lay hidden. Already she was thinking how exciting it would be when they rose out of the bushes, and faced him in quite the best "We are Hawkshaw, the detective" style.

But they had to reckon with one thing they had overlooked, and that was the collie pup. That budding genius, blundering along after his master, suddenly stopped, turned towards the fallen tree, and sniffed the air. Then he ran a few steps towards them, and stopped, his ears pricked and his eyes fixed on the tree; barked sharply, drew back a pace or two, bristled up the hair on his neck, and growled.

Red Mick turned round; "'Ello, pup," he drawled, "what's up?"

The puppy came forward again, quite close to the tree this time, and barked sharply. "Good pup," said Mick, "fitch him out, pup!—What is it—native cat? Goo for 'im!"

Thus encouraged, the puppy darted forward barking, and Red Mick stopped leisurely, picked up a large stone, and sent it crashing among the branches. It passed between Hugh and Miss Grant, and came near enough to stunning one or other of them. They jumped to their feet hurriedly, and without dignity climbed out of the branches, and advanced on Red Mick, while the puppy ran yelping behind his master.

It is only reasonable to suppose that Mick was somewhat astonished at the apparition. He could scarcely have expected his shot to disturb two such fine birds from such an extraordinary nest; but before they had extricated themselves from the branches his face had assumed the stolid, cow-like, unintelligent look which had so often baffled judges and Crown Prosecutors. He was bland and child-like as Bret Harte's Chinee.

He spoke as if he were quite accustomed to unearthing young couples out of trees. His voice had a sort of "I quite understand how it is" tone, and he spoke cheerfully.

"Good-day, Misther Hugh! Where's your horses? Have you had a fall?"

"Fall! No!" snapped Hugh, whose temper was gradually rising as the absurdity of the situation dawned on him. "We haven't had a fall. We ran the tracks of a lot of our sheep from the big paddock, and here they are now. I'd like to know what this means?"

"Is thim your sheep?" said the bland Mick, surprised. "I wuz wondherin' whose sheep they wuz, comin' up the flat. I knew they wuzn't travellin' sheep, 'cause of gettin' no notice, an me bein' laid up in the house this two days—"

"Oh, that's all very fine, Mick Donohoe?" said the young man angrily. "Your own dogs have brought them here."

Red Mick laughed gaily. "Ah, thim dogs is always yardin' up things. They never see a mob of sheep, but they'll start to dhrive 'em some place. When I was travellin' down the Darlin', goin' through Dunloe Station, in one paddock I missed th' old slut, and when I see her again, she had gethered fifteen thousand sheep, and was bringin' 'em after me. But, Lord bless your heart, Mr. Hugh," he added with a comforting smile, "she wouldn't hurt a hair of a sheep's head, nor the young dog ayther. Them sheep'll be all right. Sorra sheep ever she bit in her life. I wonder where they gethered them?"

"I'll tell you where they gathered them," said Hugh. "The fence of our paddock was dug up, and the sheep were run out, and then the fence was put up again. That's how they gathered them."

"The fence wuz dug up! Ah, look at that now. Terrible, ain't it. An' who done it, do ye think? Some of them carriers, I expect, puttin' their horses in unbeknownst to you. I'll bet 'twas them done it. Or, perhaps," he added, with an evident desire to assist in solving the difficulty, "perhaps the wind blew it down."

"What!" said Hugh scornfully. "Wind blow down a fence! What next!"

"Well it does blow terrible hard sometimes in these parts," said Red Mick, shaking his head dolefully; "look at me crop of onions I planted—the wind blew 'em out of the ground, and hung 'em on the fence. But wait now, till we have a look at these sheep."

"No, we won't wait," said Hugh angrily. "We will be off home now, and send a man for them. And I advise you to be very careful, Mick Donohoe, for I have my own idea who dug up that fence."

"Well, you don't suppose that I done it, do you?" said Red Mick. "I've been in the house this three days. Besides, I wouldn't steal my brother-in-law's sheep, anyhow. Won't ye come up, and have a dhrink of tea now, you and the lady? It's terrible hot."

"No, thank you," said Hugh stiffly. "Come along, Miss Grant." And they marched off towards the horses.

"It beats all who could have took them posts down, doesn't it?" said Mick. "I'd offer a reward, if I was you. Them fellows about here would steal the eyes out of your head. Good day to ye, Mr. Hugh."

And the cockatoo added, "Good-bye, Cockie," in a sepulchral voice, as they trudged off, smitten hip and thigh.

Hugh was suffering intensely at his defeat, and when Mary Grant said, "I suppose you will have him put in gaol at once?" he muttered that he would have to think it over. "It wouldn't do to prosecute him and fail, and we have no proof that he dug up the fence."

"But why did he say that the sheep belonged to his brother-in-law?"

Hugh started. "Did he say that? Well, he—he must have wanted to make out that he did not know whose sheep they were" but he thought to himself, "Is Red Mick going to bring up that old scandal?"

Mick, as he watched them go, winked twice to himself, and then stooped and patted the head of the collie pup. The other dogs, in answer to a silent wave of his hand, had slunk off quietly. The riders had disappeared. It had been a narrow escape, and Red Mick knew it; and even as things had turned out, there was still ample chance of a conviction.

On the way back to the homestead Hugh began to talk of the chance of a conviction, and the delight it would be to give Mick seven years, but his ideas were disturbed by thoughts of Mick's face as he said, "Why should I steal my brother-in-law's sheep?" He looked at the girl alongside him, and prayed that the old story might never be resurrected.

CHAPTER XV
A PROPOSAL AND ITS RESULTS

The question whether Mick Donohoe should be prosecuted was not likely to be prejudiced by his claim of kinship. Billy the Bully would as soon prosecute his own brother-in-law as anybody else—sooner, in fact. So Hugh, having reached home very crest-fallen and angry, wrote a full account of the affair in his report of the station work, and asked whether he should lay an information.

Grant's reply was brief and to the point; he seldom wrote letters, always telegraphing when possible. On this occasion the telegram said, "Prosecute at once; offer reward informers;" which, leaking out (as telegrams frequently did at the local office) put Red Mick considerably on the qui vive. The old man actually paid him the compliment of writing a letter about him later on, saying that it would be a good thing to prosecute—it would give Red Mick a good scare, even if it didn't get him into gaol. Circumstances, no doubt, justified a prosecution, and it was hard to see bow Mick could make a counter-move.

But that gentleman was not without resource; an anonymous letter arrived for Hugh by the mailboy, a dirty, scrawled epistle, unsigned and undated, running as follows:—

"Mr. Gordon i herd you was gone to summons Michael Donohoe for sheep stealing. You better bewar there is some seen you and that girl in the bush you will get a grate shown up and her two."

This precious epistle was signed "A Friend," and on first reading it Hugh laughed heartily; but the more he thought it over the less he liked it. It was all very well to put Red Mick in the dock, but it was evident that part of the defence would be, "How came you to be under the boughs of a fallen tree with an attractive young woman when Red Mick's dogs came up with the sheep?" At the very least they would look ridiculous; and the unknown correspondent who promised them a "grate shown up" would probably take care that the story was as highly-coloured as possible. He shuddered to think what the Donohoes would say, and heartily wished he had let Red Mick alone.

He fretted for some hours, and then decided to talk it over with the girl herself. He did not care to let Red Mick think that the anonymous letter had stopped the prosecution; at the same time, he was determined to do nothing that would cause Miss Grant the least annoyance. He opened the discussion that evening while strolling about the garden.

"About this business of Red Mick's," he said. "I am rather worried."

"Why?"

"Well, the trouble is this: I've got an anonymous letter from Red Mick or some of his people, saying that they are going to give you and me a great showing-up about being hidden in the tree together."

"What can they say?" she asked, uncomprehendingly.

"Well, of course, they will talk about our being in the tree together—and—all that kind of thing, you know. They will make things as unpleasant for us as they can. They may want you to give evidence, and all that sort of thing—and I thought, perhaps you mightn't like it."

She froze into dignity at once. "I certainly shouldn't like it," she said. "About being in the tree, that does not matter, of course, but I hope you will keep my name out of the affair altogether. I must ask you to do that for me."

Then he rushed on his fate. Many a time he had pictured how he would wait till they were alone together in the garden on some glorious moonlit night, and he would take her hand, and tell her how much he loved her; and now, seeing the girl standing before him flushed with insulted dignity, he suddenly found himself gasping out, in what seemed somebody's else's voice, "Couldn't we—look here, Miss Grant, won't you be engaged to me? Then it won't matter what they say."

He tried to take her hand, but she drew back, white to the lips.

"No, no; let me go; let me go," she said. Then the colour came back to her face, and she drew herself up, and spoke slowly and cuttingly:

"I thank you very much for what you have just said. But I really think that I shall be able to put up with anything these people may choose to say about me. It won't hurt me, and I shouldn't like you to sacrifice yourself to save me from the talk of such people. Let us go back to the house, please."

He stared helplessly at her, and could not find his voice for a moment. At last he blurted out:

"It's not because of that. I don't care about them any more than you do. Don't think it's that, Miss Grant. Why—"

"Let us go back to the house, please," she said quietly, "and don't say anything more about it. And whatever happens, I must ask you to keep my name out of the affair altogether. You'll do that, won't you? Let us go back now, if you don't mind."

They walked back in silence. He looked at her once or twice, but her face was stern and rigid, and she would not give him even one glance. At the door she gave him her hand, with a matter-of-fact "I will say goodnight now," and disappeared into her room, where she threw herself on the bed and sobbed bitterly; for the truth was that she was very, very fond of him. She, too, had built her little castles in the air as to what she would say and do when he put the momentous question. Girls do foresee these things, somehow; although they do pretend to be astonished when the time arrives.

She had pictured him saying all sorts of endearing things, and making all sorts of loving protestations; and now it had come to this—she had been asked as if it were merely a matter of avoiding scandal. It was too great a shock. She lay silently crying, while Hugh, his castles in the air having crumbled around him, was trying in a dazed way to frame a letter to Mr. Grant.

His thoughts were anything but pleasant. What a fool he had been, talking to her like that! Making it look as if he had only proposed to her because he ought to protect her good name! Why hadn't he spoken to her before—in the tree, on the ride home, any other time? Why hadn't he spoken differently? To him the refusal seemed the end of all things. He thought of asking Mr. Grant to give him the management of the most out-back place he had, so that he could go away and bury himself. He even thought of resigning his position altogether and going to the goldfields. Red Mick and his delinquencies seemed but small matters now; and, after what had passed, he must, of course, see that Miss Grant was not dragged into the business. So he sat down and began to write.

The letter took a good deal of thinking over. It had got about the station that Red Mick had at last been caught *in flagrante delicto;* the house-cook had told the cook at the men's hut, and he had told the mailman, who stopped on the road to tell the teamsters ploughing along with their huge waggons to Kiley's Crossing; they told the publican at Kiley's, and he told everybody he saw. The children made a sort of play out of it, the eldest boy personating Red Mick, while two of the younger ones hid in a fallen tree, and were routed out by Thomas Carlyle. The station-hands were all excitement; the prospect of a big law-case was a real godsend to them. To drop the matter would be equivalent to a confession of defeat, but, after what had passed, Hugh had no option. So he told Mr. Grant that, on thinking it over, he did not consider it advisable to go on with the case against Red Mick; Miss Grant would have to go into the box to give evidence, which would be very unpleasant for her.

Poor Hugh! He was too honourable to give any false reason, and too shy to tell the whole truth. If he had said that there was no hope of a conviction, it would have been all right. But consideration for the feelings of anyone, even his own daughter, was to Billy the Bully quite incomprehensible, and he wrote back, on a letter-card, "Go on with the prosecution."

This put Hugh in a frightful dilemma. He had no trouble whatever in making up his mind to disobey the order, as he was bound to stand by his promise to Miss Grant. But what answer should he send to her father? He was in a reckless mood, but he knew well enough that Grant would order him off the place, neck and crop, if he dared to disobey; and he owed it to his mother and sister to avoid such a thing. The more he looked at the position of affairs, the less he liked it. He wrote a dozen letters, and tore them up again.

He thought of making Red Mick a sporting offer of, say, a couple of hundred pounds, to disappear altogether—Mick could have arranged that easily enough. Then he thought of going down to see Mr. Grant to explain; but the more he thought of that the less he liked it. He worried and worried over it, and when he went to bed lay awake thinking about it. He fell into dozes, and dreamt that Mr. Grant had turned him off the place, and had made Red Mick manager, and that Miss Grant was going to marry Red Mick; then he woke with a start, and heard through the darkness the rapid hoof-beats of a horse ridden at speed up the road from Kiley's, and the barking of dogs that announced the arrival of a stranger.

He went out and found in the yard one of the telegraph operators from Kiley's, on a smoking horse. "Very important telegram, Mr. Gordon," he said. "I borrowed the horse, and brought it over as fast as I could."

Hugh opened the envelope hurriedly. The operator struck a match and held it up while he read. The message was from the secretary of Grant's club, and ran as follows:

"William Grant died suddenly this morning. Pinnock taking charge of affairs; am making arrangements funeral. Better come down at once."

Her father dead! The question of Red Mick and his prosecution became at once a matter of no moment. How absurd his worry and vexation now seemed. On the other hand, what new complications might arise? All these years the Gordons had lived on the assumption that Mr. Grant would provide for them, without having any promise or agreement from him; and, owing to the old man's violent temper, they had been in daily risk of being ordered off the place. They had got used to this as people get used to living on the side of a volcano. But now—?

Her father dead! He could not bear to see her grief, and the thought of it made him determined to get away as quickly as possible. Quietly he awoke his mother, and told her what had happened, and by dawn was well on his way to Tarrong to catch the train to Sydney.

CHAPTER XVI
THE ROAD TO NO MAN'S LAND

Now we must follow for a time the adventures of Charlie Gordon and the new chum, whom we left just starting out for 'far back', Charlie to take over a cattle-station for Old Man Grant, and Carew to search for Patrick Henry Considine. After a short sea-journey they took train to a dusty back-blocks township, where Gordon picked up one of the many outfits which he had scattered over the country, and which in this case consisted of a vehicle, a dozen or so of horses, and a black boy named Frying Pan.

They drove four horses in a low, American-made buggy, and travelled about fifty miles a day. Frying Pan was invaluable. He seemed to have a natural affinity for horses. He could catch them anywhere, and track them if they got lost. Carew tried to talk to him, but could get little out of him, for he knew only the pidgin English, which is in use in those parts, and said "No more" to nearly every question. He rode along behind the loose horses, apparently quite satisfied with his own company. Every now and then he came alongside the vehicle, and said "Terbacker." Charlie threw him a stick of the blackest, rankest tobacco known to the trade, and off he went again.

Once they saw him get off his horse near a lagoon, plunge his arm into a hole, and pull out a mud-turtle, an evil-smelling beast; this he carried for several miles over his shoulder, holding its head, and letting the body swing at the end of the long neck—a proceeding which must have caused the turtle intense suffering. After a while his horse shied, and he dropped the turtle on the ground with a dull thud.

"Aren't you going to pick him up again?" cried Carew.

"No more," replied Frying Pan, carelessly. Then he grinned, and volunteered a remark. "Make that feller plenty tired walk home again," he said. And this was his only conversation during a two-hundred-mile journey.

At night they usually managed to reach a station, where the man in charge would greet them effusively, and beg them to turn their horses out and stay a week—or a year or two, just as long as they liked. They met all sorts at these stations, from English swells to bushmen of the roughest.

Sometimes they camped out, putting hobbles on the horses, and spreading their blankets under the buggy on a bed of long grass gathered by Frying Pan.

As they got further out, the road became less and less defined, stations fewer, and everything rougher. They left the sheep-country behind them and got out into cattle-land, where "runs" are measured by the hundred square miles, and every man is a law unto himself. They left their buggy after a time, and pushed on with pack-horses; and after travelling about two hundred miles, came to the outer edge of the settled district, where they stayed with two young Englishmen, who were living under a dray, and building their cattle-yards themselves—the yards being a necessity, and the house, which was to come afterwards, a luxury. The diet was monotonous—meat "ad libitum," damper and tea. They had neighbours within sixty miles, and got letters once in two months by riding that distance. "Stay here a while," they said to the travellers, "and take up some of the country near by."

"We're to take over the country Redman took up," said Charlie. "It joins you doesn't it?"

"Yes. See those far blue ranges? Well, we run to them on this side, and Redman's block runs to them on the other."

"Don't your cattle make out that way?" asked Charlie.

"No fear," replied he, laughing. "We've some good boundary riders out there."

"What do you mean?"

"The wild blacks," answered the Englishman. "They're bad out on those hills. You'll find yourselves in a nice shop when you take that block over. There's a pretty fair humpy to live in, that's one thing. What do you call the place?"

"No Man's Land."

"Good name, too," said the other. "It's not fit for any man. I wish you'd stop with us a while, but I suppose we'll see you coming back."

"I suppose so," said Charlie. "We won't be there longer than we can help. Who's on the block now? Redman sold his rights in it after he'd mortgaged it to my uncle."

"There's old Paddy Keogh there now—greatest old character in the North. Lives there with his blacks and a Chinaman. Regular oldest-inhabitant sort of chap. Would have gone with Noah in the Ark, but he swore so badly they wouldn't have him on board. You'll find him great fun."

"I suppose he'll give us possession all right. We don't want any trouble."

"He'd fire at you just as soon as look at you, I think," said the other. "But I don't fancy he wants to stay there much. It's not the first time he's been broke, so I don't expect he'll take it very hard. Well, if you won't stay, good-bye and good luck! Give my best wishes to old Paddy."

They resumed the weary journey, and after another two days' riding sighted away over the plain a small iron house, gleaming in the setting sun. "Here we are!" said Charlie. "That's No Man's Land."

The arrival was not inspiring. They rode their tired horses up to the low-roofed galvanised-iron house, that looked like a huge kerosene-tin laid on its side, with a hole cut for a door and two holes for windows. There was no garden and no fenced yard. It was stuck down in the middle of the wilderness, glaring forlornly out of its windows at a wide expanse of dry grass and dull-green bushes. Behind it was a small duplicate, which served as kitchen and store. A huge buffalo-head was nailed to a tree near by. In front was a rail on which were spread riding-saddles, pack-saddles, hobbles, surcingles, pannikins, bridles, empty bags, and all manner of horse-gear; and roundabout were a litter of chips, an assortment of empty tins, bits of bullock-hide, empty cartridge-cases, and the bare skulls of three or four bullocks, with neat bullet-holes between the eyes.

Amidst this congenial *debris* roamed a herd of gaunt pigs, fierce-eyed, quarrelsome pigs, that prowled restlessly about, and ever and again returned disconsolately to the stinking carcasses of some large birds of prey that had been thrown out in the sun. They were flat-sided, long-legged, long-nosed, and had large bristling manes—showed, in fact, every sign of reverting to the type of the original pig that yachted with Noah. Living with them, in a state of armed neutrality, were three or four savage-looking cattle dogs, who honoured the strangers with deep growls, not condescending to bark.

Charlie pulled up in front of the house, and cooeed. A Chinaman put his head out of the kitchen door, smiled blandly, said "'Ello!" and retired. Gordon and Carew unsaddled the horses, put the hobbles on, and carried all the gear into the house. By this time the Chinee had donned a dirty calico jacket, and began in silence to put some knives, forks, and pannikins on the table.

"Where's the old man?" roared Charlie, as if he thought the Chinee were deaf.

"No more," he replied.

"Don't understand any English, eh?"

"No more," said he.

Just then a tramping of hoofs was heard; and looking out of the back door they saw, about two hundred yards away, a large horse-yard, over which hung a cloud of dust. Under the dust were signs of a struggle.

"He's in the yard," said Charlie. "Let's go up."

The cloud of dust shifted from place to place, and out of it came a medley of weird oaths, the dull thudding of a waddy, and the heavy breathing of men and animals in combat. Suddenly a lithe, sinewy black boy, dressed in a short blue shirt, bounded like a squirrel to the top of the fence and perched there; and through the mist they saw a very tall old man, holding on like grim death to the end of a long rope, and being hauled about the yard in great jumps by a half-grown steer. Behind the steer another black boy dodged in and out, welting and prodding it from time to time with a bamboo pole. Maddened by the blows, the steer would dash forward and narrowly miss impaling the man on his horns; then, taking advantage of his impetus, the old man would try to haul him into a smaller yard. Every time he got to the gate the steer yanked him out again by a series of backward springs that would have hauled along a dromedary, and the struggle began all over again. The black boy on the fence dropped down with the agility of a panther, took up the rope behind the old man, and pulled for all he was worth.

"Hit him there, Billy! Whack him! Come on, you son of a cow! I'll pull you in if I have to pull your head off. Come on, now!" And once more the struggle raged furiously.

Charlie clambered up on the fence and sat there for a moment. The old man saw him, but evinced no surprise. He just said, "Here, Mister Who-ever-you-are, kitch hold of that rope." Their united forces were too much for the steer, and he was hauled in by main strength under a fusillade of bamboo on his stern. Once in the small yard, he abandoned the struggle, and charged wildly at his captors. The old man slipped nimbly to one side, Gordon darted up the nearest fence, while Carew and the black boy got tangled up with the rope.

In the sauve qui peut which ensued, Carew pushed the black down on the ground right in front of the steer, which immediately fell over him, and tangled him up more than ever. Then it turned on him with a roar of rage, butted him violently, rolled him over and over in the dirt, knelt on him, bellowed in his ear, and slobbered on him. It looked as if the boy must be killed. His mate dashed in with a bamboo, and welted and whacked away without making any impression, till the animal of its own accord withdrew gloomily to a corner of the yard, dragging the rope after it. Carew watched the prostrate boy in agonised suspense, hardly daring to hope that he was alive. With a gasp of satisfaction he saw him rise to his feet, rub some of the dirt off his face, and look round at the steer. Then he gave his shirt a shake and began to brush himself with his hands, saying in an indignant tone, "Flamin' bullock! Spoil my new chirt!"

Now all hands seized the rope again; in a trice the bullock was hauled up against the fence, thrown to the ground, and held there while the old man sawed off the point of one horn, which was growing into the animal's eye. When the job was done he straightened himself up, and through the covering grime and dust they had a good look at him.

He had a long, red nose, a pair of bright hazel eyes, and a bushy, grizzled beard and moustache hiding all the lower part of his face. On his head was a shapeless felt hat, from which a string passed under his nose. His arms were hairy and baboon-like; his long thin legs seemed intended by Nature to fit the sides of a horse. He wore tweed pants, green with age, and strapped on the inside with a lighter-coloured and newer material; also a very dirty coloured cotton shirt, open in front, and showing a large expanse of hairy chest. His voice was husky from much swearing at profligate cattle, and there was a curious nasal twang in his tone, a sort of affectation of Americanism that was a departure from the ordinary bush drawl.

Charlie introduced himself. "My name's Gordon," he said, "and this is a friend of mine. We've come to take this block over."

"You're welcome to it, Mister," said the old man promptly. "It's about broke me, and if you don't look out it'll break you. Any man that gits this place will hump his swag from it in five years, mark me! Come on down to the house," he continued, picking up the rope and other gear lying about the fence. "Now, you boys, let that steer out, and then go and help the gins bring the cattle in. Look lively now, you tallow-faced crawlers. Come on, Mister. Did you bring any square-face with you?"

"We brought a drop o' rum," replied Charlie.

"Ha! That'll do. That's the real Mackay," said the veteran, slouching along at a perceptibly quicker gait.

"But, look, see here now, Mister!" he continued, anxiously, "you didn't let Ah Loy get hold of it, did you? He's a real terror, that Chow of mine. Did you see him when you came in?"

"Yes, we saw him. He couldn't speak any English, seemingly."

"That's him," said the old man. "That's him! He don't savvy much English. He knows all he wants, though. He can lower the rum with any Christian ever I see. It don't do to let him get his hands on a bottle of anythink in the spirit line. It'll come back half-empty. Now then, cook," he roared, seating himself at the rough slab table, and drumming on it with a knife, "let's have some grub, quick, and you'll get a nip of rum. This new boss b'long you, you savvy. All about station b'long him. I go buffalo-shooting. Me stony broke. Poor fellow me! Been fifteen years in this God-forgotten country, too," he said reminiscently, placing his elbows on the table, and gazing at the wall in front of him. "Fifteen years livin' mostly with the blacks and the Chineyman, and livin' like a black or a Chineyman, too. And what have I got to show for it? I've got to hump my bluey out of this, and take to the road like any other broken-down old swagman."

"It's a bit rough," said Charlie. "How did you come to grief?"

"Oh, I came out here with a big mob of cattle," said the old man, filling his pipe, as Ah Loy placed some tin plates, a tin dish, and a bottle of Worcester sauce on the table, and withdrew to the kitchen for the provender. "I lived here, and I spent nothing, and I let 'em breed. I just looked on, and let 'em breed. Oh, there was no waste about my management. I hadn't an overseer at two pounds ten a week, to boss a lot of flash stockmen at two pounds. I jest got my own two gins and three good black boys, and I watched them cattle like a blessed father. I never saw a stranger's face from year's end to year's end. I rode all over the face of the earth, keepin' track of 'em. I kep' the wild blacks from scarin' 'em to death, and spearin' of 'em, as is their nature to, and I got speared myself in one or two little shootin' excursions I had."

"Shooting the blacks?" interpolated Gordon.

"Somethin' like that, Mister. I did let off a rifle a few times, and I dessay one or two poor, ignorant black feller-countrymen that had been fun' my cattle as full of spears as so many hedgehogs—I dessay they got in the road of a bullet or two. They're always gettin' in the road of things. But we don't talk of shootin' blacks nowadays These parts is too civilised—it's risky. Anyhow, I made them blacks let my cattle alone. And I slaved like a driven nigger, day in and day out, brandin' calves all day long in the dust, with the sun that hot, the brandin' iron 'ud mark without puttin' it in the fire at all. And then down comes the tick, and kills my cattle by the hundred, dyin' and perishin' all over the place. And what lived through it I couldn't sell anywhere, because they won't let tick-infested cattle go south, and the Dutch won't let us ship 'em north to Java, the wretches! And then

Mr. Grant's debt was over everything; and at last I had to chuck it up. That's how I got broke, Mister. I hope you'll have better luck."

While he was delivering this harangue, Carew had been taking notes of the establishment. There was just a rough table, three boxes to sit on, a meat safe, a few buckets, and a rough set of shelves, supporting a dipper and a few tin plates, and tins of jam, while in the corner stood some rifles and a double-barrelled gun. Saddlery of all sorts was scattered about the floor promiscuously.

Certainly the owner of No Man's Land had not lived luxuriously. A low galvanised-iron partition divided the house into two rooms, and through the doorway could be seen a rough bunk made of bags stretched on saplings.

As the old man finished speaking, Ah Loy brought in the evening meal — about a dozen beautifully tender roast ducks in a large tin dish, a tin plate full of light, delicately-browned cakes of the sort known as "puftalooners," and a huge billy of tea. There were no vegetables; pepper and salt were in plenty, and Worcester sauce. They ate silently, as hungry men do, while the pigs and cattle-dogs marched in at the open-door, and hustled each other for the scraps that were thrown to them.

"How is it the pigs have no tails?" asked Carew.

"Bit off, Mister. The dogs bit them off. They've got the ears pretty well chawed off 'em too."

Just then a pig and a dog made a simultaneous rush for a bone, and the pig secured it. The dog, by way of revenge, fastened on to the pig, and made him squeal like a locomotive engine whistling. The old man kicked at large under the table, and restored order.

"You ain't eatin', Mister," he said, forking a duck on to Carew's plate with his own fork. "These ducks is all right. They're thick on the lagoon. The Chow only had two cartridges, but he got about a dozen. He lays down and fires along the water, and they're floatin' very near solid on it. But here's the cattle comin' up."

Looking out of the door, they saw about two hundred cattle coming in a long, stringing mob up the plain, driven by four black figures on horseback. As they drew near the yards, several cattle seemed inclined to bolt away; but the sharp fusillade of terrific whips kept them up to the mark, and, after a sudden halt for a few minutes, the mob streamed in through the gates. A number of rails were put in the posts, and made fast with pegs. The riders then remounted, and came cantering and laughing down to the homestead. All four were aboriginals, two were the boys that had been seen at the yard. The two new boys were dressed in moleskins, cotton shirts, and soft felt hats, and each had a gaudy handkerchief tied round his throat.

One was light, wiry, and graceful as a gazelle—a very handsome boy, the embodiment of lightness and activity. The other was short and squat, with a broad face. Both grinned light-heartedly as they rode up, let their horses go, and carried their saddles on to the verandah, without bothering about the strangers.

"Those are nice-looking boys," said Carew. "I mean the two new boys just coming in."

"New boys!" said the old man. "Them! They're my two gins. And see here, Mister, you'll have to keep off hangin' round them while you're camped here. I can't stand anyone interferin' with them. If you kick my dorg, or go after my gin, then you rouse all the monkey in me. Those two do all my cattle work. Come here, Maggie," he called, and the slight "boy" walked over with a graceful, easy swing.

"This is new feller?" he said, introducing Carew, who bowed gracefully. "He b'long Sydney. You think him plenty nice feller, eh?"

"Yowi," said the girl laughing. "He nice feller. You got 'em matches?" she said, beaming on Carew, and pulling a black pipe out of her trousers' pocket. "Big fool that Lucy, drop 'em matches."

Carew handed over his match-box in speechless amazement.

"They've been out all day with the cattle," said the old man. "I've got a lot of wild cattle in that there mob. I go out with a few quiet ones in the moonlight, and when the wild cattle come out of the scrubs to look at 'em we rush the whole lot out into the plain. Great hands these gins are—just as good as the boys."

"Good Lord!" said Carew, looking at the two little figures, who had now a couple of ducks each, a puftalooner or two, and a big pannikin of tea, and were sitting on the edge of the verandah eating away with great enjoyment; "what have they been doing with the cattle to-day?"

"Minding them lest the wild ones should clear out. They dropped their matches somehow; that's what fetched 'em home early. They'll have to sleep on the verandah to-night. We'll make that their boodore, as they say in France."

The dark was now falling; the sunlight had left long, faint, crimson streaks in the sky. The air was perceptibly cooler, and flights of waterfowl hurried overhead, making their way to the river. The Chinaman lighted a slush-lamp, by whose flickering light Charlie produced from his swag a small bundle of papers, and threw them on the table.

"We might as well get our business over, Keogh," he said. "I've got the paper here for you to sign, making over your interest in the block and the cattle, and all that."

He pored over the document, muttering as he read it. "Your name'll have to be filled in, and there's a blank for the name of the person it's transferred to."

"That'll be Mr. Grant's name," suggested Carew.

"I don't know so much about that," said Charlie. "I don't think, if a man has a mortgage over a place, that he can take it in his own name. That fool Pinnock didn't tell me. He was too anxious to know how we got on with the larrikins to give me any useful information. Anyhow, I'll fill in my own name—for all the block is worth I ain't likely to steal it. I can transfer it to Mr. Grant afterwards."

"I don't care," said the old man indifferently, "I'll transfer my interest to anyone you like. I'm done with it. I'm signing away fifteen of the best years of my life. But my name ain't Keogh, you know, though I always went by that. My father died when I was a kiddy, and my mother married again, so I got called by my stepfather's name all my life. This is my right name, and it's a poor man's name to-day." And as the two men bent over him in the light of the flickering slush-lamp, he wrote, with stiff, uncertain fingers, "Patrick Henry Considine."

CHAPTER XVII
CONSIDINE

For a few seconds no one spoke. Carew and Gordon stared at the signature, and then looked at each other. The newly-found Considine looked at his autograph in a critical way, as if not quite sure he had spelled it right, and then stood up, handing the deed to Gordon.

"There y'are," he said. "There's my right, title and intrust in all this here block of land, and all the stock what's on it; and if you're ever short of a man to look after the place in the wet season I'll take the job. I might be glad of it."

"I think it's quite likely you won't want any job from me," said Charlie. "I'll be asking you for a job yet. Are you sure that's your right name? What was your father?"

"My name? O' course it's my name. My father was billiard-marker at Casey's Hotel, Dandaloo," said the old man with conscious pride. "A swell he had been, but the boose done him up, like many a better man. He used to write to people over in England for money, but they never giv him any."

"Where did he write to?" asked Carew, looking at the uncouth figure with intense interest. "Do you know what people he wrote to?"

"Yairs. He wrote to William Considine. That was his father's name. His father never sent any money, though. Told him to go to hell, I reckon."

"What was your father's name?"

"William Patrick Considine."

Carew dashed out to his saddle, hurriedly unstrapped a valise, and brought in a small packet of papers.

"Here you are," he said, opening one, and showing it to Gordon. "Those are the names, Patrick Henry Considine, son of William Patrick Considine. Entitled under his grandfather's will—by Jove, do you know there's a lot of money waiting for you in England?"

"There's what?"

"A lot of money left you. In England. Any amount of it. If you are the right man, you're rich, don't you know. Quite a wealthy man."

"How much money d'you say, Mister?"

"Oh, a great deal. Thousands and thousands. Your grandfather left it. No one knew for certain where you were, or if you were alive."

"I'm alive all right, I believe," said Considine, staring hard at them. "But look, Mister—you aren't trying to take the loan of me? Is this straight?"

"Yes, it's straight," said Charlie. "You'll have to go to England to make your claim good, I expect. It's straight enough. That's what brought Mr. Carew out here, to try and find you."

For some time the bushman smoked in silence, looking at each man in turn, perhaps expecting them to laugh. He muttered once or twice to himself under his breath. Then he turned on Gordon again.

"Now, look here, Mr. Gordon, is this square? Because, if it ain't, it'll be a poor joke for some of you!"

"Man alive, why should we want to fool you? What good could it do us? It's all right."

"Well, if it's all right, we'll all have a drink on it. Here, Maggie, Lucy, Billy, come here. Get it pannikin. You won't mind me treatin' 'em with your rum, I suppose, Mister?" he said, turning to Gordon. "I don't come in for a fortune every day, you know, and there ain't a drop of lush in the place, only yours."

"Fire away," said Charlie.

"Come on, Lucy. Come on, Maggie. Where's Ah Loy? Watch their faces, Mister, it's as good as a play. Now then, ladies, I bin poor fella longa teatime, now rich feller longa bedtime. You savvy?"

The gins grinned uncomprehendingly, but held out their pannikins, and into each he poured a three-finger nip of raw overproof rum that would have burnt the palate of Satan himself. They swallowed it neat, in two or three quick gulps. The tears sprang to their eyes, and they contorted their faces into all sorts of shapes; but they disdained to take water after it.

"My word, that strong feller, eh?" said Considine. "Burn your mouth, I think it. Now then, Ah Loy, how much you wantee? That plenty, eh?"

Ah Loy peered into the tin pannikin with a dejected air, and turned it on one side to show that there wasn't much in it.

"Here y'are, then," said his boss. "Have a bit more. We don't come in for a fortune every day. Watch him take it, Mister."

Ah Loy put the fiery spirit to his lips, and began to drink in slow sips, as a connoisseur sips port wine.

"Good heavens," said Carew, "it'll burn the teeth out of his head."

The Chinee sipped away, pausing to let the delicate fluid roll well into the tender part of his mouth and throat.

"Welly stlong!" he said at last; but he finished the lot. The two black boys had their share, and retired again to their camp. Then the three white men sat out in front of the house on some logs, smoking, and looking at the blazing stars.

Considine had fifty questions to ask, and the more Carew tried, the more helpless it was to explain things to him.

"D'you say there's a house left me with this here money?"

"Yes," replied Carew. "Beautiful old place. Old oaks, and all that sort of thing. You'll like it, I'm sure. Used to be a pack of hounds there."

"Ha!" said Considine with contempt. "I don't think much of this huntin' they have in England. Why, I knew a chap that couldn't ride in timber a little, and he went to England and hunted, and d'you know what he said? He said he could have rode in front of the dogs all the way, if he'd have liked. But the owner of the dogs asked him not to, so he didn't."

"I suppose I could take Maggie and Lucy there," he went on, looking doubtfully at his hearers. "They wouldn't mind a chap havin' a couple of black lady friends, would they? Yer see, they've stuck with me well, those two gins, and I wouldn't like to leave 'em behind. They'd get into bad hands. They're two as good handy gins as there is in the world. That little fat one—you start her out with a bridle and enough tobacker after lost horses, and she'll foller 'em till she gets 'em, if it takes a week. Camps out at night anywhere she can get water, and gets her own grub—lizards and young birds, and things like that. There ain't her equal as a horse-hunter in Australia. Maggie ain't a bad gin after horses, but if she don't find 'em first day, she won't camp out—she gets frightened. I'd like to take 'em with me, yer know."

As he spoke the two moleskin-trousered, cotton-shirted little figures passed in front of the hut. "There they go," he said. "Two real good gins. Now, as man to man, you wouldn't arst me to turn them loose, would you?"

Carew looked rather embarrassed, and smoked some time before answering.

"Well, of course," he said at last, "they'd put up with a good deal from you, bein' an Australian, don't you know. Fashion just now to make a lot of fuss over Australian chappies, whatever they do. But two black women—rather a large order. You might get married over there, and then these two black ladies—"

He was interrupted by a startled exclamation from Considine. "Married!" he said. "Married! I forgot all about my wife. I am married!"

"What!" said Charlie. "Are you married?"

"Yairs. Married. Yairs! Should just think I was."

"Not to a lubra, I suppose?"

"Lubra, no! A hot-tempered faggot of a woman I met at Pike's pub. I lived with her three weeks and left her there. I haven't seen her this six years."

"Did you and she have some er—differences, then?" said Carew.

"Differences? No I We had fights—plenty fights. You see, it was this way. I hadn't long got these two gins; and just before the rains the wild geese come down in thousands to breed, and the blacks all clear out and camp by the lagoons, and kill geese and eat eggs and young ones all day long, till they near bust. It's the same every year—when the wild geese come the blacks have got to go, and it's no use talkin'. So I was slavin' away here—out all day on the run with the cattle—and one night I comes home after being out three days, and there at the foot of the bunk was the two gins' trousers and shirts, folded up; they'd run away with the others.

"So I goes after 'em down the river to the lagoons, and there was hundreds of blacks; but these two beauties had heard me coming, and was planted in the reeds, and the other blacks, of course, they says, "No more" when I arst them. So there I was, lonely. Only me and the Chinaman here for two months, 'cause his gin had gone too. So one day I ketches the horses, and off I goes, and travels for days, till I makes Pike's pub, and there was this woman.

"It seems from what I heard afterwards that she'd just cleared out from some fellow she'd been livin' with for years—had a quarrel with him. Anyhow, I hadn't seen a white woman for years, and she was a fine lump of a woman, and I got on a bit of a spree for a week or so, you know—half-tight all the time; and it seems some sort of a parson—a mish'nary to the blacks—chanced along and married us. She had her lines and everything all right, but I don't remember much about it. So then I'm living with her for a bit; but I don't like her goin's on, and I takes the whip to her once, and she gets snake-headed to me, and takes up an axe; and then one day comes a black from this place and he says to me, he says, "Old man," he says,

"Maggie and Lucy come back." So then I says to my wife, "I'm off back to the run," I says, "and it's sorry I am that ever I married you." And she says, "Well, I'm not goin' out to yer old run, to get eat up with musketeers." So says I, "Please yourself about that, you faggot," I says, "but I'm off." So off I cleared, and I never seen her from that day till this. I married her under the name of Keogh, though. Will that make any difference?"

This legal problem kept them occupied for some time; and, after much discussion, it was decided that a marriage under a false name could hardly be valid.

Then weariness, the weariness of open-air, travelling, and hard work, settled down on them, and they made for the house. On the verandah the two gins lay sleeping, their figures dimly outlined under mosquito nets; the dogs crouched about in all sorts of attitudes. Considine turned in all standing in the big rough bunk, while Carew and Gordon stretched their blankets on the hard earth floor, made a pillow of their clothes, and lay down to sleep, after fixing mosquito nets. Gordon slept as soon as he touched the blankets, but Carew tumbled and tossed. The ground was deadly hard. During the journey Frying Pan had got grass for their beds; here he had not been told to get it, and it would have looked effeminate to ask for grass when no one else seemed to want it. The old man heard him stirring and rolling, and sat up in his bunk. "What's up, Mister?" he said kindly. "D'you find it a hard camp?"

"Not too easy," said the Englishman. "Always seems to be a deuced hard place just under your hip, don't you know?"

"I'll put you right in a brace of shakes," said Considine. "I've got the very thing to make a soft bed. Half a minute now, and I'll get it for you."

He went out to the back of the house, and returned with a dry white bullock-hide, as rigid as a sheet of iron. This he threw down at Carew's feet.

"Here y'are, Mister; put that under you for a hipper, and you'll be all right."

Carew found the hide nearly as hard as the bare floor, but he uttered profuse thanks, and said it was quite comfortable; to which the old man replied that he was sure it must be, and then threw himself back on his bunk and began snoring at once. But Carew lay long awake.

CHAPTER XVIII
THE WILD CATTLE

Carew awoke next morning to find that it was broad daylight, and the horses had been run in, caught, and saddled, all ready for a start to the run. Breakfast was soon disposed of, and the cavalcade set out. Naturally, the old man had heaps of questions to ask about his inheritance, and made the Englishman ride alongside while he questioned him.

"If I go to England after this money, Mister, I suppose they won't be handin' me out ten years for perjury, same as they done for Roger Tichborne, eh? I won't have no law case, will I?"

"Shouldn't think so. You've been advertised for all over the place, I believe."

"Ha! Well, now they've got me they mightn't like me, don't you see? I never took no stock in them unclaimed-money fakes. I never see any money goin' beggin' yet, long as I've lived, but what some chap had his hands on it quick enough. But I s'pose it's all right."

"It's me wife I'm troublin' about. I'm no dandy, Goodness knows, but if people'll let me alone I'll let them alone, and I don't interfere with anyone. But if old Peg turns up she'll want to be right in front of the percession. If she follows me, I'll realise everything by public auction, unreserved sale, for spot cash, and I'll sneak back here to a place I knows of, where there's no trooper can find me. I ain't goin' halves with that woman, I tell you. She wouldn't stick to me if I was poor, and I ain't goin' to take her up again now. You'd better come back with me, Mister, and show me the way round a bit."

"There's a mob of cattle, Gordon." he went on, changing the subject quickly; "let's ride up here, while the boys bring 'em into camp." And off they went at a carter, leaving the question of his social prospects in abeyance for the time being.

The ceremony of taking delivery lasted some days, Considine's signature to the deed of transfer being only the first step. This long document, prepared in Sydney, kept them going in literature for about a week; and they were delighted to find that, through the carelessness of a clerk, in one part of the deed there figured "one bull of mixed sexes and various ages."

They rode out, day after day, through interminable stretches of dull timbered country, or over blazing plains waving with long grass. Here they came on mobs of half-wild cattle, all bearing the same brand, a huge RL5. These were not mustered into a yard or counted, except roughly. Gordon was not completing a purchase, but simply taking over what were there—many or few; good or bad, he could only take what he found.

Miles and miles they rode, always in the blazing heat, camping for a couple of hours in the middle of the day. To the Englishman it seemed always the merest chance that they found the cattle, and accident that they got home again. At rare intervals they came upon substantial mustering-yards, where the calves were brought for branding; near these a rough hut had been constructed, so that they could camp there at night, instead of returning to the head station.

They always slept out of doors. In the intense heat it was no hardship, and the huts, as a rule, fairly jumped with fleas. Once they camped alongside a big lagoon, on whose surface were huge pink and blue water-lilies and rushes, and vast flocks of wild fowl. After the stretches of blazing plain and dull timber this glimpse of water was inexpressibly refreshing.

On their way back they struck new country, great stretches of almost impenetrable scrub, tropical jungle, and belts of bamboo. In this cover wild cattle evidently abounded, for they frequently heard the bellow of the bulls.

"There should be a terrible lot of wild cattle here," said Charlie. "Don't you ever get any out of the scrubs?"

"Oh, yes, we moonlight for 'em." said Considine. "We take coachers out. We have a very fair coaching mob. Some of our coachers are as quick as racehorses, and they'll hustle wild cattle away from the scrub just as if they understood."

"What do you mean by coachers?" asked Carew. "Not cattle that go in carts, eh?"

"Carts, no. The way we get wild cattle here-abouts is to take out a mob of quiet cattle, what we call coachers, and let 'em feed in the moonlight alongside the scrub, while we wait back out o' the road and watch 'em. When the wild cattle come out, they run over to see the coachers, and we dash up and cut 'em off from the scrub, and hustle 'em together into the open. It's good sport, Mister. We might try a dash at it, if you like, before we go back; it's moonlight now."

"Let's have a try to-night" said Gordon. "Are your coachers handy?"

"Yairs. They feed near the house. I'll send 'em on with the gins to-night."

When they got back that evening, Carew was so dead-tired that he wished the wild cattle expedition at Jericho. But Considine and Charlie were in great form, directing, arguing, and planning the expedition. One of the black boys rode out, and returned driving a big mob of horses that dashed into the yard at full gallop. The gins and the black boys caught fresh mounts out of these and started away, driving some fifty head of cattle selected from a mob that made their headquarters within a few miles of the house. Most of them were old stagers, and strung away in the evening quite tranquilly, while the blacks, always smoking, rode listlessly after. Considine produced two stockwhips, and gave one to Charlie.

"No good givin' you one. Mister," he said to Carew. "You'd hang yourself with it most likely. I've got a rare good horse for you—old Smoked Beef. He'd moonlight cattle by himself, I believe. You'd better have a pistol, though."

"What for?" asked Carew, as Considine produced three very heavy navy revolvers and a bag of cartridges.

"To shoot any beast that won't stay with the mob. Some of 'em won't be stopped. They have to go. Well, if one goes, the rest keep trying to follow, and no forty men will hold 'em. You just keep your eyes open, and if a beast breaks out in spite of the whips, you shoot him if the blacks tell you. See?"

"Where am I to shoot him?"

"Shoot him any place. In the earhole, or the shoulder, or the ribs, or the flank. Any place at all. Shoot him all over if you like. One or two bullets don't hurt a beast. It takes a lead-mine to kill some of 'em."

"Do the blacks shoot?" asked Charlie.

"No, I don't never trust no blacks with firearms. One boy knifes well, though. Races alongside and knifes 'em."

This seemed a fairly difficult performance; while the Englishman was wondering how it would be carried out, they made a start. They rode mile after mile in the yellow moonlight, until they discerned a mob of cattle feeding placidly near some big scrub. They whistled to the blacks, and all rode away down wind to a spot on the edge of the plain, a considerable distance from the cattle.

Here they dismounted and waited, Considine and Charlie talking occasionally in low tones, while the blacks sat silent, holding their horses. Carew lay down on the long dry grass and gazed away over the plain. His horse stood over him with head down, apparently sleeping. Far away under the moon, in vague patches of light and shade, the cattle were feeding. Hours seemed to pass, and Carew almost fell asleep.

Suddenly a long-drawn bellow, the angry challenge of a bull, broke the silence. A mob of wild cattle were evidently coming along the edge of the scrub, and had caught scent of the strangers. Again the bull roared; there is no animal on earth with so emphatically warlike a note as the wild bull when advancing to meet a strange mob. The quiet cattle answered with plaintive, long-drawn lowings, and the din became general as the two lots met.

"Let 'em get well mixed up," said Considine quietly, tightening his girths, and swinging into the saddle. Everyone followed his example. Carew was shaking with excitement. Angry bellowing now arose from the cattle, which were apparently horning one another—such being their manner of greeting.

Considine said, "There's a big lot there. Hope to blazes we can hold 'em. Are you ready, Mister?"

"Yes, I'm ready," replied Carew.

"Come on, then. We'll sneak up slowly at first, but once I start galloping let your horse go as fast as he likes, and trust him altogether. Don't pull him at all, or he'll break your neck."

They started slowly in Indian file, keeping well in the shadow of the scrub. The horses picked their way through the outlying saplings and bushes, until suddenly Considine bent forward on his horse's neck, and said, "Come on!"

What a ride that was! The inexperienced reader is apt to imagine that because a plain is level, it is smooth, but no greater fallacy exists. The surface of a plain is always bad galloping. The rain washes away the soil from between the tussocks, which stand up like miniature mountains; the heat cracks the ground till it opens in crevices, sometimes a foot wide and a yard or two deep; fallen saplings lie hidden in the shadows to trip the horse, while the stumps stand up to cripple him, and over all is the long grass hiding all perils, and making the horse risk his own neck and his master's at every stride.

They flew along in the moonlight, Considine leading, Charlie next, then the two black boys, and then Carew, with a black gin on each side of him, racing in grim silence. The horses blundered and "peeked," stumbled, picked themselves up again, always seeming to have a leg to spare. Now and again a stump or a gaping crack in the ground would flash into view under their very nose, but they cleared everything—stumps, tussocks, gaps, and saplings.

In less time than it takes to write, they were between the mob and the scrub; at once a fusillade of whips rang out, and the men started to ride round the cattle in Indian file. The wild ones were well mixed up with the tame, and hardly knew which way to turn. Carew, cantering round, caught glimpses of them rushing hither and thither—small, wiry cattle for the most part, with big ears and sharp, spear-pointed horns. Of these there were fifty or sixty, as near as Considine could judge—three or four bulls, a crowd of cows and calves and half-grown animals, and a few old bullocks that had left the station mobs and thrown in their lot with the wild ones.

By degrees, as the horses went round them, the cattle began to "ring," forming themselves into a compact mass, those on the outside running round and round. All the time the whips were going, and the shrill cries of the blacks rang out, "Whoa back! Whoa back, there! Whoa!" as an animal attempted to break from the mob. They were gradually forcing the beasts away from the scrub, when suddenly, in spite of the gins' shrill cries, some of the leaders broke out and set off up the plain; with the rush of a cavalry charge the rest were after them, racing at full speed parallel with the edge of the scrub, and always trying to make over towards it.

Old Considine met this new development with Napoleonic quickness. He and the others formed a line parallel with the course of the cattle, and raced along between them and the timber, keeping up an incessant fusillade with their whips, while the old man's voice rang out loudly in directions to the blacks behind.

"Keep the coachers with 'em! Flog 'em along! Cut the hides off 'em!"

In the first rush the quiet cattle had dropped to the rear, but the blacks set about them with their whips; and, as they were experienced coachers, and had been flogged and hustled along in similar rushes so often that they knew at once what was wanted, they settled down to race just as fast as the wild ones. As the swaying, bellowing mass swept along in the moonlight, crashing and trampling through the light outlying timber, some of the coachers were seen working their way to the lead, and the wild cattle having no settled plan, followed them blindly. Considine, on his black horse, was close up by the wing of the mob, and the others rode in line behind him, always keeping between the cattle and the scrub.

"Crack your whips!" he yelled. "Crack your whips! Keep 'em off the scrub! Go on, Billy, drive that horse along and get to the lead!"

Like a flash one of the black boys darted out of the line, galloped to the head of the cattle, and rode there, pursued by the flying mob, the cracks of his heavy stockwhip sounding above the roar of hoofs and the bellowing of the cattle. Soon they steadied a little, and gradually sobered down till they stopped and began to "ring" again.

"That was pretty pure, eh, Mister?" roared Considine to Carew. "Ain't it a caution the way the coachers race with 'em? That old bald-face coacher is worth two men and a boy in a dash like this."

Suddenly an old bull, the patriarch of the wild herd, made towards one of the gins, whose shrill yells and whip-cracking failed to turn him. Considine dashed to her assistance, swinging his whip round his head.

"Whoa back, there! Whoa back, will you!" he shouted. The bull paused irresolute for a second, and half-turned back to the mob, but the sight or scent of his native scrub decided him. Dropping his head, he charged straight at Considine. So sudden was the attack that the stock-horse had barely time to spring aside; but, quick as it was, Considine's revolver was quicker. The bull passed—bang! went the revolver, and bang! bang! bang! again, as the horse raced alongside, Considine leaning over and firing into the bull's ribs at very short range.

The other cattle, dazed by the firing, did not attempt to follow, and at the fourth shot the bull wheeled to charge. He stood a moment in the moonlight, bold and defiant, then staggered a little and looked round as though to say, "What have you done to me?" Bang went the revolver again; the animal lurched, plunged forward, sank on his knees, and fell over on his side, dead.

"There, you swab," said the old man, "that'll larn you to break another time." Then he took once more his place in the patrol round the mob. They circled and eddied and pushed, always staring angrily at the riders. Suddenly a big, red bullock gave a snort of defiance, and came out straight towards Carew. He stopped once, shook his head ominously, and came on again. One of the gins dashed up with the whip; but the bullock had evidently decided to take all chances, and advanced on his foes at a trot.

"Choot him, that feller!" screamed the gin to Carew. "You choot him! He bin yan away! No more stop! Choot him!"

Carew lugged out his revolver, and tried to pull his horse to a standstill, but the wary old veteran knew better than to be caught standing by a charging bullock; just as Carew fired, he plunged forward, with the result that the bullet went over the mob altogether, and very nearly winged Charlie, who was riding on the far side. Then the bullock charged in earnest;

and Carew's horse, seeing that if he wished to save human life he must take matters into his own hands, made a bolt for it. Carew half-turned in the saddle, and fired twice, only making the black boys on the far side cower down on their horses' necks. Then the horse took complete charge, and made off for the scrub with the bullock after him, and every animal in the mob after the bullock.

Nothing in the world could have stopped them. Considine and Charlie raced in front, alongside Carew, cracking their whips and shouting; the blacks flogged the coachers up with the wild cattle; but they held on their way, plunged with a mighty crash into the thick timber, and were lost. No horseman could ride a hundred yards in that timber at night. Coachers and all were gone together, and the dispirited hunters gathered at the edge of the scrub and looked at each other.

"Well, Mister, you couldn't stop him," said the old man.

"I'm afraid I made—rather a mess of things, don't you know," said the Englishman. "I thought I hit him the second time, too. Seemed to be straight at him."

"I think you done very well to miss us! I heard one bullet whiz past me like a scorpyun. Well, it can't be helped. Those old coachers will all battle their way home again before long. Gordon, I vote we go home. They're your cattle now, and you'll have to come out again after 'em some day, and do a little more shootin'. Get a suit of armour on you first, though."

As they jogged home through the bright moonlight, they heard loud laughter from the blacks, and Carew, looking back, found the fat gin giving a dramatic rehearsal of his exploits. She dashed her horse along at a great pace, fell on his neck, clutched wildly at the reins, then suddenly turned in her saddle, and pretended to fire point-blank at the other blacks, who all dodged the bullet. Then she fell on the horse's neck again, and so on *ad lib*.

This made the Englishman very morose. He was quite glad when Charlie said he had seen enough of the cattle, and they would all start next day for civilisation—Charlie to resume the management of Mr. Grant's stations, Carew to go with him as "colonial experiencer," and Considine to start for England to look after his inheritance.

CHAPTER XIX
A CHANCE ENCOUNTER

The black boys went in with them to Pike's store to take back supplies on the pack-horse. They travelled over the same country that they had seen coming up; the men at the stations greeted them with the same hospitality. Nothing was said about Considine's good fortune. It was thought wise to be silent, as he didn't know how soon his wife might hear of it.

They left the gins at the blacks' camp, which they chanced on by a riverside. The camp was a primitive affair, a few rude shelters made by bending bamboo sticks together and covering them with strips of paper bark. Here the sable wariors sat and smoked all day long, tobacco being their only civilised possession. Carew was very anxious to look at them, a development of curiosity that Considine could not understand.

"Most uninteresting devils, I call 'em," he said. "They're stark naked, and they have nothing. What is there to look at?"

Having parted with Maggie and Lucy, they pushed onwards, the old man beguiling the time with disquisitions on the horse-hunting capabilities of his gins, whom he seemed really sorry to leave. As they got near Pike's, he became more restless than ever.

"See here, Mister," he said at last, "my wife's here, I expect, and if she gets wind of this, I'll never get rid of her. The only thing to do is to slip away without her knowing, and she might never hear of it. I won't go into the place at all. I'll go on and camp down the creek, and get the coach there after it leaves the town, and she'll never know."

The town of "Pike's" consisted of a hotel, a store, a post-office, a private residence, and coach-stables; these were all combined in one establishment, so the town couldn't be said to be scattered. Pike himself was landlord of the "pub," keeper of the store, officer in charge of the post-office, owner of the private residence, holder of the mail contract, and proprietor of the coach-stables. Behind him was only wilderness and "new" country.

Nobody ever saw him at home. Either he was on the road with a bullock-team, bringing up supplies for the hotel and store, or he was droving cattle down on a six months' journey to market; or he was away looking at new country, or taking supplies out to men on the half-provisioned stations of the "outer-back;" or else he was off to some new mining camp or opal-field, to sell a dray-load of goods at famine prices.

When Charlie and Carew rode up to the store they did not see Pike, nor did they expect to see him. By some mysterious Providence they had arrived the very day the coach started on its monthly trip down to Barcoo; and in front of the hotel were congregated quite a number of people—Pike's wife and his half-wild children, a handful of bushmen, station hands, opal miners, and what-not, and last, but not least, a fat lady of about forty summers, with flaring red hair.

She was a fine "lump" of a woman, with broad shoulders, and nearly the same breadth all the way down to her feet. She wore a rusty black dress, which fitted perilously tight to her arms and bust; on her head was a lopsided, dismantled black bonnet with a feather—a bonnet that had evidently been put away in a drawer and forgotten for years. Any want of colour or style in her dress was amply made up for by the fact that she positively glowed with opals. Her huge, thick fingers twinkled with opal rings; from each of her ears there dangled an opal earring the size of a form; her old dress was secured round her thick, muscular neck by a brooch that looked like an opal quarry, and whenever she turned to the sun she flashed out rays like a lighthouse.

Her face was fat and red, full of a sort of good-humoured ferocity; she moved like a queen among the bystanders, and shook hands gravely with each and all of them. She was hot, but very dignified. Evidently she was preparing to start in the coach, for she packed into the vehicle with jealous care a large carpet-bag of garish colouring that seemed to harmonise well with the opals. While she was packing this away, Charlie and Carew went into the store, and bought such supplies as were needed for the establishment at No Man's Land. Gordon took the opportunity to ask the shock-headed old storekeeper, Pike's deputy, some questions about the lady, who was still scintillating between the coach and the house, carrying various small articles each trip.

"Don't yer know 'er?" said the man, in much the same tone that Bret Harte's hero must have used when he was so taken aback to find that a stranger—

"Didn't know Flynn,—
Flynn of Virginia."

"Don't yer know 'er?" he repeated, pausing in his task of scooping some black cockroachy sugar from the bottom of a bin. "That's the Hopal Queen! She's hoff South, she is. Yer'll be going in the coach, will yer?"

"Yes," said Charlie. "We're going in the coach. There's no extra fare for travelling with such a swell, is there? Where on earth did she get all those opals?"

"Ho, blokes gives 'em to 'er, passin' back from the hopal fields. In the rough, yer know! Hopal in the rough, well, it's 'ard to tell what it'll turn out, and they'll give 'er a 'unk as sometimes turns out a fair dazzler. She's a hay-one judge of it in the rough, too. If she buys a bit of hopal, yer bet yer life it ain't a bad bit when it's cut. What about these 'ere stores? Goin' to take 'em with yer?"

"No," said Charlie. "The black boy is here for them. He's going to take them back with him."

"What, Keogh's black boy! Well, I don't know as Pike'll stand old Paddy Keogh any longer. Paddy's 'ad a dorg tied hup 'ere" (*i.e.*, an account outstanding) "this two years, and last time Pike was 'ome 'e was reck'nin' it was about hup to Keogh to pay something."

"They're not for Keogh," said Charlie. "They're for me. I've taken Keogh's block over."

The old man looked at him dubiously.

"Well, but y'aint goin' to tie hup no dorg on us for 'em, are yer? I s'pose it's all right, though?"

"Right, yes," said Gordon. "It's for Mr. Grant, Old Man Grant,—you've heard of Grant of Kuryong?"

"Never 'eard of him," said the aged man, "but it makes no hodds. Pay when yer like. Yer'd better git on the coach, for I see the Hopal Queen's ready for a start. Yer'll know her all right before long, I bet. Some of the fellers from round about 'as come in to give her a send-off like. There's the coach ready; yer'd better git aboard, and yer'll hear the-the send-off like. Young Stacy out there reckons 'e's going to make a speech."

Charlie and Carew climbed upon the coach. The fat lady kissed Pike's wife and children with great solemnity. "Good-bye, Alice! Good-bye, Nora darlin'," she said. Then she marched in a stately way towards the vehicle, with the children forming a bodyguard round her. A group of men hung about uneasily, looked sheepish, and waved large, helpless red hands, till a young fellow about seven feet high—who looked more uneasy and had even larger hands than the rest—was hustled forward, and began to mutter something that nobody could hear.

"Speak up, George," said a friend. The young man raised his voice to a shout, and said—

"And so I propose three cheers and long life to the Hopal Queen!"

As he spoke he ran two or three paces forward towards a stump, meaning, no doubt, to get on it and lead the cheering; but, just as he was going to jump, a wretched little mongrel that had been in and out among the people's feet made a dash at him, fixed its teeth in the calf of his leg, and ran away howling at its own temerity. The young giant rushed after it, but the Opal Queen interposed.

"George," she said, "don't ye dare go for to kick my dog!"

"Well, what did he bite me for, then?" said the giant, speaking out now in a voice that could be heard half a mile off. "What did he bite me for?"

"Never mind, George! Don't ye go for to kick him, that's all."

The Opal Queen, snorting like a grampus, climbed into the coach; the driver cracked his whip, and off they went, leaving the audience spellbound, and the gigantic young man rubbing his leg. Soon Pike's faded away in the distance. As the coach jolted along, Carew and Charlie on the box seat occasionally peered in at the large swaying figure, half-hidden in the dust.

About two miles out of town Considine, with all his earthly belongings in a small valise, stopped the coach and got on board, sitting in front with them.

"Have a look inside," said Charlie. "There's a woman in there looks rather like—the lady you were talking about."

Considine looked in. Then he sank back in his seat, with a white face. "By Heavens!" he said, "it's my wife."

"This is funny," said Charlie. "Wonder what she's after. She must have heard, somehow. She'll never lose sight of you, now, Considine."

Here the driver struck into the conversation. "See her inside?" he said, indicating the inside passenger with a nod of his head. "She's off to Sydney, full rip. She reckons her husband's dead, and she's came in for a fortune."

"Oh, she reckons he's dead, does she?" said Charlie carelessly. "Didn't know she had a husband."

"Ho yes," said the driver. "She came up here passin' by the name of Keogh, but it seems that ain't her husband's name at all."

"Oh, indeed! Do you happen to have heard what her husband's name is? And when did he die?"

"I never heard the noo husband's name," replied the driver. "Keogh was *her* name. I dessay if I arst her she'd tell me. Shall I arst her?" "No," said Considine firmly. "Don't annoy her at all. Leave well alone, young feller. What odds is it to you how many husbands the poor woman has had?"

"No," said the driver dispassionately. "It's no odds to me, nor yet to you, I don't suppose. She's in for a real big thing, I believe. A telegram came to the telegraph station after I left last trip, and young Jack Sheehan, he brought it on after me — rode a hundred miles pretty well, to ketch me up. He reckoned she was coming in for a hundred thousand pounds. I wouldn't mind marryin' her meself, if it's true; plenty worse-looking sorts than her about. What do you think, eh, Mister?" addressing Considine.

"Marry her, and be blowed," said that worthy, sociably; and the driver stiffened and refused to talk further on the subject.

Meanwhile the three discussed the matter in low tones. It was practically impossible that anyone could have heard of the identity of Keogh with the missing Considine. How then had the story got about that her husband was dead, and that she had come into money? She must have seen Considine get on the coach, but she had made no sign. Their astonishment was deeper than ever when the coach stopped for a midday halt. It was quite impossible for Considine to conceal himself. The house, where the coach changed horses, was a galvanised-iron, one-roomed edifice in the middle of a glaring expanse of treeless plain, in which a quail could scarcely have hidden successfully. It was clear that Considine and his wife would have to come face to face.

Carew and Charlie looked expectantly at each other, and clambered down quickly when the coach stopped. Considine descended more slowly; straightening his figure and looking fixedly before him, he marched up to the door of the change-house.

His wife got leisurely out of the coach, put on her bonnet, and walked straight over to him; then she looked him full in the face for at least three seconds, and passed by without a sign of recognition.

The three men looked at each other.

"Well, this bangs all," said Considine. "She knew me all right. Why didn't she speak? She's afraid I'll clear out, and she's shammin' not to know me, so's she'll have me arrested as soon as she sights a bobby. I know her. Perhaps I'd better offer her something to go back and leave me alone, hey?"

This was vetoed by a majority of two to one, and once more the coach started. They plodded away on the weary, dusty journey, until the iron roofs and walls of Barcoo gleamed like a mirage in the distance, and the coach rolled up to the hotel. A telegraph official came lounging forward.

"Anyone here the name of Charles Gordon?" he said.

"That's me," said Charlie.

"Telegram for you," he said. "It's been all over the country after you."

Gordon tore it open, read it, and stood spellbound. Then he silently handed it to Carew. It was several weeks old, and was from Pinnock, the solicitor. It read as follows—"William Grant died suddenly yesterday. Will made years ago leaves everything to his wife. Reported that he married Margaret Donohoe, and that she is still alive. Am making all inquiries. Wire me anything you know."

Charlie's face never changed a muscle.

"That's lively!" he said. "He never married that woman; and, if he did, she died long ago."

As he spoke, the lady passenger, having had some talk with the hotel people, came over to him with a beaming smile. "And ye're Charlie Gordon," she said with a mellifluous mixture of brogue and bush-drawl. "An' ye don't know me now, a little bit? Ye were a little felly when we last met. I'm Peggy Donohoe that was—Peggy Grant now, since I married poor dear Grant that's dead. And, sure, rest his sowl!"—here she sniffed a little—"though he treated me cruel bad, so he did! Ye'll remember me brother Mick—Mick with the red hair?"

"Yes," said Charlie, slowly and deliberately, "I remember him well; and you too. And look here, Peggy Donohoe—or Peggy Keogh, whichever you call yourself—you and Red Mick will have the most uphill fight you ever fought before you get one sixpence of William Grant's money. Why, your real husband is here on the coach with us!"

He turned and pulled Considine forward, and once more husband and wife stood face to face. Considine, alias Keogh, smiled in a sickly way, tried to meet his wife's eyes, and failed altogether. She regarded him with a bold, unwinking stare.

"Him!" she said. "Him me husban'! This old crockerdile? I never seen him before in me life."

A look of hopeless perplexity settled on Considine's features for a moment, and then a ray of intelligence seemed to break in on him. She repeated her statement.

"I never seen this man before in me life. Did I? Speak up, now, and say, did I?"

Considine hesitated for a moment in visible distress. Then, pulling himself together, and looking boldly from one to the other, he replied—

"Now that you mention it, ma'am, I don't think as ever you did. I must ha' made some mistake."

He walked rapidly away, leaving Gordon and Peggy face to face.

"There y'are," she said, "what did I tell ye? Husban'? He's no husban' o' mine. Ye're makin' a mistake, Charlie."

Charlie looked after the retreating bushman, and back at the good lady who was beaming at him.

"Don't call me Charlie," he said. "That old man has come in for a whole lot of money in England. His name is Considine, and he pretends he isn't your husband so that he can get the money and leave you out of it. Don't you be a fool. It's a lot better for you to stick to him than to try for William Grant's money. Mr. Carew and I can prove he said you were his wife."

"Och, look at that now! Said I was his wife! And his name was Considine, the lyin' old vaggybond. His name's not Considine, and I'm not his wife, nor never was. Grant was my husban', and I'll prove it in a coort of law, so I will!" Her voice began to rise like a south-easterly gale, and Charlie beat a retreat. He went to look for the old man, but could not find him anywhere.

Talking the matter over with Carew he got no satisfaction from the wisdom of that Solon. "Deuced awkward thing, don't you know," was his only comment.

Things were even more awkward when the coach drew up to start, and no sign of the old man could be found. He had strolled off to the back of the hotel, and vanished as absolutely as if the earth had swallowed him.

The Chinese cook was severely cross-questioned, but relapsed into idiotic smiles and plentiful "No savee's". A blackfellow, loafing about the back of the hotel, was asked if he had seen a tall, thin old man with a beard going down the street. He said, "Yowi, he bin go longa other pub;" but as, on further questioning, he modified his statement by asserting that the man he saw was young, short and very fat, no heed was paid to his evidence—it being the habit of blacks to give any answer that they think will please the questioner.

"He'll play us some dog's trick, that old fellow," said Charlie. "I can't wait here looking for him, though. I'll find him when I want him if he's above ground. Now let's go on. Can't keep the coach waiting for ever while we unearth him. Let's get aboard."

Just as the coach was about to start a drover came out of the bar of the hotel, wiping his lips with the back of his hand. He stared vacantly about him, first up the street and then down, looked hard at a post in front of the hotel, then stared up and down the street again. At last he walked over, and, addressing the passengers in a body, said, "Did any of you's see e'er a horse anywheres? I left my prad here, and he's gorn."

A bystander, languidly cutting up a pipeful of tobacco, jerked his elbow down the road.

"That old bloke took 'im," he said. "Old bloke that come in the coach. While yous was all talking in the pub, he sneaks out here and nabs that 'orse, and away like a rabbit. See that dust on the plain? That's 'im."

The drover looked helplessly out over the stretch of plain. He seemed quite incapable of grappling with the problem.

"Took my horse, did he? Well, I'm blowed! By Cripes!"

He had another good stare over the plain, and back at the party.

"My oath!" he added.

Then the natural stoicism of the bushman came to his aid, and he said, in a resigned tone,

"Oh, well, anyways, I s'pose—s'pose he must have been in a hurry to go somewheres. I s'pose he'll fetch him back some time or other."

Gordon leant down from the box of the coach.

"You tell him," he said, "when he does fetch him back, that if I'd had a rifle, and had seen him sneaking off like that he'd have wanted an ambulance before he got much farther. Tell him I'll find him if I have to hunt him to death. Tell him that, will you?"

"All right, Mister!" said the drover, obligingly, "I'll tell him!"

The horses plunged into their collars; off went the coach into long stretches of dusty road, with the fat red lady inside, and our two friends outside. And in course of time they found themselves once more in Sydney, where they took the earliest opportunity to call on Pinnock, and hold a council of war against Peggy.

CHAPTER XX
A CONSULTATION AT KILEY'S

Within twenty-four hours after Peggy got back to her old home, it was known all over the mountains that she meant business, and would make a claim on William Grant's estate. Rumour, of course, supplied all the needful details. It was said, and even sworn to, that Peggy had her marriage lines put by in a big iron box, ready to be produced at the proper time. Other authorities knew for a fact that she had no proofs, but that the family at Kuryong were going to give her any sum from a thousand pounds to a million, to cancel her claim and save exposure.

As a matter of fact, none of those who talked knew anything whatever. Peggy confided in no one but Red Mick, and that worthy had had enough legal experience of a rough and ready sort to know that things must be kept quiet till the proper time. But by way of getting ready for action Red Mick and his sister one fine morning rode up to Gavan Blake's office to consult him as to what they should do.

Blake was not at all surprised to see them. He, of course, had heard all the rumours that were afloat, and knew that if Peggy brought forward any claim he would be asked to act for her professionally. He had not quite decided whether he would act or not. In his hard commonsense mind he saw next to no possibility of Peggy having a *bonâ fide* case. He did not suppose for a moment that William Grant would have run his neck into a bigamy noose; and it would put the young lawyer in a very awkward position with Mary Grant if, after saving her life and posing as her friend, he carried on a blackmailing suit against her. At the same time, he felt that it could do no harm to either side to investigate Peggy's case; there might be awkward things that he could help to suppress. So with expectancy and not a little amusement he saw his clients ride up and tie their horses to the fence outside his office, and watched Peggy straighten her ruffled plumage before entering.

They came in at the door with a seriousness worthy of the occasion. Peggy heaved a subdued sigh and settled in a chair. Red Mick opened the conversation.

"Mornin' to you, Gavan," he said.

By virtue of his relationship Mick was privileged to call his brilliant nephew by his Christian name. To the rest of the clans Gavan was Mr. Blake.

"Good-morning, Mick. Good-morning, Peggy. Have you had any rain?"

In the bush no one would think of introducing discussion without a remark about the weather.

"Jist a few drops," said Red Mick gloomily. "Do us no good at all. Things is looking terrible bad, so they are. But we want to see ye—" and here he dropped his voice, rose, and cautiously closed the door—"Peggy here, Mrs. Grant, d'ye see,"—Mick got the name out without an effort—"she wants to see ye about making a claim on the estate. 'Tis time she done somethin'. All these years left to shift for herself—"

Here Blake broke in on him. He meant to probe Peggy's case thoroughly, and knew that it would be no easy matter to get at the truth while she had Red Mick alongside to prompt her. He had not dealt with the mountain folk for nothing, and handled his clients in a way that would astonish a more conservative practitioner.

"Mick," he said, "You go over to Isaacstein's store and wait till I send for you."

"I want Mick to be wid me," began Peggy.

Blake blazed up. He knew that he must keep his ascendancy over these wild people by force of determination.

"You heard what I said," he thundered, turning fiercely on Peggy. "You want this and you want that! It's not what you want, it's what *I* want! You do what you're told. If you don't—I won't help you. Mick, you go over to the store, and wait till I send for you." And Mick shambled off.

Peggy, still inclined to be defiant, settled herself in her chair. She had battled in North Queensland so long that she neither feared nor respected anybody; but her native shrewdness told her she had all to gain and nothing to lose by doing what her lawyer advised.

"Now, Peggy," he said, "do you want to make a claim against William Grant's estate?"

"Yis."

"On the ground that you're his widow?"

"Yis. I'll tell yer—"

"No, you won't tell me anything. I'll tell *you*. If you are to have any hope of succeeding in this case, you must furnish me with the name of the priest or parson who married you, the place where you were married, and the date. It must be a real priest or parson, a real place, and a real date. It's no use coming along with a story of a marriage by a parson and you've forgotten his name, at a place you can't remember where it was, and a date that's slipped your memory. You must have a story to tell, and it must hold water. Now, can you tell such a story? Have you got any proofs at all?"

Peggy shifted about uneasily.

"Can I see Mick?" she said.

"No, you can not. You must out with it here and now. Listen to me, Peggy," he went on, sinking his voice suddenly and looking hard at her. "I've got to know all about this. It's no use keeping anything back. Were you ever married to William Grant?"

Peggy dropped her voice too.

"Yis. I was married twenty-five years ago at a place called Pike's pub, out in the Never-never country."

"Who read the service, parson or priest?"

"Neither. A mish'nary. Mish'nary to the blacks."

"Is he alive?"

"No, he died out there. He was sick then, wid the Queensland fever."

"What was his name?"

"Mr. Nettleship."

"Was the marriage ever registered?"

"Sorra one of me knows. He giv us each a bit of paper—our marriage lines. 'Twas written in pencil. He had no ink in the place, and he had no books wid him. He tore the sheet of paper and give us each half, wid the writing on it; his horses got stole and he had to camp there. He stayed round wid Pike and the blacks till he died."

"And where is the certificate? Have you lost it?"

"I sint mine down to Mick to keep for me—jist a bit of paper written in pencil it was—and it got lost some ways; but I have a copy of it I med at the time."

"Where is the copy now?"

"At Mick's place."

"You must tell Mick to bring it in. Now where is this place, Pike's?"

"Out this side of the opal-fields. It's wild and rough now, but what it was then—well 'twas more like a black's camp nor a white man's place at all."

Blake thought the story had gone far enough. He did not believe a word of it. "Look here, Peggy," he said, "You have given the place, the date, the name of the parson, and everything. Now you know that if you are telling a lie it will be easily found out. They will soon find out if there was such a missionary, and if he was up there at the time, and if Mr. Grant was up there; and if you are caught out in a lie it may go hard with you. Have you any witnesses?"

"Martin Doyle was there, Black Martin's son."

"What! Martin Doyle that's out at the nine-mile?"

"Yis. He was up driving the buggy and horses for Grant. He can swear to the wedding.

"He can."

"Yis."

Blake sat back in his chair and looked at her. "Do you mean to tell me," he said, "that you can show me a certificate and a witness to your marriage with William Grant?"

Peggy looked doggedly down at the floor and said, in the tones of one who is repeating the burial service or some other solemn function, "I can prove the marriage."

Blake was puzzled. He had known the mountain folk all his life, and knew that for uneducated people—or perhaps because they were uneducated people—they were surprisingly clever liars. But he never dreamt that any of them could hoodwink him; so he put Peggy once more through the whole story,—made her describe all her actions on the day of the wedding, where she stood, where the witness stood, what the parson said, what her husband said. He went through the whole thing, and could see no flaw in it. He knew that Peggy would not scruple to lie to him; but, with the contempt of a clever man, he felt satisfied that he could soon upset any concocted story. This story seemed to hold water, and the more he cross-examined her the more sure he was that there was something genuine about it; at the same time, he was sure that it was not all genuine. Then a thought occurred to him.

"Would you settle this case if they offered you something?" he said.

"I'll do whatever you say," said Peggy, rising. "'Tis for you to say what I ought to do. 'Tis not for the like of me, that is no scholar."

"Leave it to me," said Blake. "I'll do what is best for you. Send Martin Doyle in to see me, Martin that was the witness. And about this copy of the certificate, tell Mick to bring it in here. Now you go home, and don't you say to one living soul one word of what has passed in here. Tell them you are going on with the case, but don't say any more, or you may land yourself in gaol. Do you hear me?"

And the cowed and flustered Peggy hurried away to join her brother, who was far too wise to ask questions.

"Least said soonest mended," he said, when told that Blake required silence.

After his clients had gone, Gavan Blake sat for half an hour almost dazed. If Peggy's story was true, then Mary Grant was an outcast instead of a great heiress. And while he had become genuinely fond of her (which he never was of Ellen Harriott), he had no idea of asking her to share his debts with him. He puzzled over the affair for a long time, and at last his clear brain saw a way out of all difficulties. He would go over to the old station, put the whole case before Mary Grant, and induce her for peace' sake to give Peggy money to withdraw her claim. Out of this money he himself would keep enough to pay all his pressing debts. He would be that much to the good whatever happened, and afterwards would have an added claim on Mary Grant's sympathies for having relieved her of a vast lawsuit in which her fortune, and even her very name, were involved.

This plan seemed to him the best for all parties—for himself especially, which was the most important thing. If he could get a large sum to settle the case, he could make Peggy give him a big share for his trouble, and then at last be free from the haunting fear of exposure and ruin. He felt sure that he was doing quite right in advising Mary Grant to pay.

Again and again he ran over Peggy's case in his mind, and could see no flaw in it. In the old days haphazard marriages were rather the rule than the exception, and such things as registers were never heard of in far-out parts. His trained mind, going through the various questions that a cross-examiner would ask, and supplying the requisite answers, decided that, though it might seem a trifle improbable, there was nothing contradictory about Peggy's story. A jury would sympathise with her, and the decisions of the Courts all leaned towards presuming marriage where certain circumstances existed. By settling the case he would do Mary Grant a real kindness. And afterwards—well, she would probably be as grateful as when he had saved her life. He saw himself the hero of the hour: ever prompt to decide, he saddled a horse, and at once rode off to Kuryong to put the matter before her.

CHAPTER XXI
NO COMPROMISE

While Gavan Blake was conferring with his clients, a very different sort of conference was being held at Kuryong. The return of Charlie Gordon, accompanied by Carew, had been voted by common consent an occasion for holiday; and although, according to theory, a bush holiday is invariably spent in kangaroo-hunting, yet the fact is that men who are in the saddle from daylight to dark, from week-end to week-end, generally spend a holiday resting legs that are cramped from the saddle, and arms that ache from lifting sheep over hurdles or swinging the gates of drafting-yards.

Thus it was that, on the holiday at Kuryong, the Bachelors' Quarters—two large dormitory-like rooms that opened into one another—were full of athletic male figures sprawling on the beds, smoking black pipes all day, and yarning interminably. The main topic of conversation was Peggy's claim against the estate. They had all heard the rumours that were going round; each had quietly been trying to find out what Peggy had to go on, and this pow-wow was utilised for the purpose of comparing notes. They had one advantage over Gavan Blake—they knew all about Considine, which Blake did not.

On one bed lay Pinnock, who had come up to make arrangements for carrying on the station till the will was proved. On another bed sprawled Carew, who, by virtue of his trip out back, was looked upon as a bit of an oracle by Poss and Binjie, who had never been further than the mountains. Poss and Binjie had dragged an old couch out of the next room and were stretched on that, listening to the talk, and occasionally throwing in a word of such wisdom as they had. Hugh sat in an armchair by the window, smoking and dreaming.

Poss's voice cut knife-like through a cloud of tobacco smoke. He spoke as one on the defensive.

"Well, I believe there's something in it, anyhow. Briney Donohoe told me—"

Charlie Cordon's cold drawl interrupted the youth. "It's all rot," he said. "Briney Donohoe told you—what does *he* know about it? You two boys and Hugh have been stuck at home here so long, you believe anything. I tell you, they'll do nothing. It's all talk, just to make themselves big people. They have nothing to do just now, so it comes in handy as an excuse to ride from one selection to another all day long and leave our gates open. We have Peggy's measure, haven't we, Carew? That long-lost relation of yours, old Considine!"

"I wish you did have him," said the lawyer. "He might come in very handy. With a big property like this to go for, they are nearly sure to have a try at it."

Poss took heart at finding himself supported by this new champion. "Yes," he said. "Red Mick and Peggy are down at Gavan Blake's to-day. I saw their horses hanging up outside as I came through. And Briney Donohoe told me—"

"What do you think, Carew?" said Charlie, cutting Briney Donohoe off again. "Don't you think that old fellow was telling the truth when he said he married Peggy?"

"Sure he was," said the Englishman. "Never saw a fellow in such a funk in my life."

"What about Peggy?" said Pinnock. "How did she take it?"

"Bold as brass! I thought she was going to kiss Charlie there, when she found out who he was."

Pinnock laughed. "Funny thing," he said, "a woman like Peggy having the chance to choose between two fortunes. Pity we couldn't induce her to take the old bushman and be done with it. How much money has he come into, Carew?"

"Oh, plenty of money. But of course there's an old place to keep up, and the death duties are very heavy. Very expensive thing having money left you in England, you know."

Charlie Gordon turned to Pinnock. "What you ought to do," he said (the far-out man who has to shift for himself is always quite sure he can settle all difficulties better than those whose profession it is), "what you ought to do," he repeated, "is to send someone to Peggy and tell her not to be such a fool. Tell her to stick to old Considine. That's what you ought to do."

"Well, suppose *you* go and do it. You know the lady better than anyone here, seemingly. But if she has been to see Blake, I expect the fat's in the fire by this time."

"I don't think much of Blake takin' up the case," said Binjie, "after the old lady asked him here. It's doing the black-snake act, I call it. I don't suppose he'll come here any more after this."

Hugh still sat looking out of the window, smoking silently. "Here comes Blake now, anyhow," he said. "He's just coming up the flat."

"Wants to see me, I expect," said Pinnock. "We'll know all about it now. Must have heard I was here, and is come to declare war or sue for peace. Someone had better go and meet him, I suppose."

"Dashed if I'll go," said Poss. "I don't care about a chap that doesn't act white. I saw Red Mick's and Peggy's horses at his office to-day, and now he comes up here as bold as brass."

"Let him go round to the front," said Hugh, "and then he can ask the servants for whoever he wants. If we go out and meet him, we'll have to ask him to stay."

The approach to houses in the bush is generally by way of the yard where the horses arrive, and it is very unusual for anyone, except a stranger making a formal visit, to be allowed to find their way round to the front.

Blake rode up and gave his horse to the horse-boy. "Put him in the stable for a while," he said. "I may want him again." Then he went round to the front door and asked for Mrs. Gordon.

"I have come to see Miss Grant on very important business," he said when the old lady came in. "Would you ask her if she would see me?"

The old lady was in a quandary. She had heard all the rumours that were going about, but she knew that they had been kept from Mary Grant, and she thought that if Blake meant to talk business he might shock or startle the girl terribly.

"Mr. Pinnock the lawyer is here," she said. "Perhaps you had better see him. Miss Grant does not know—"

"I am come as a friend of Miss Grant's, Mrs. Gordon," he said. "But, if Mr. Pinnock is here, perhaps it would be better for me to see him first. Shall I wait for him here?"

"If you will go into the office I will send him in there," and the old lady withdrew to talk of commonplace matters with Mary, all the time feeling that a great crisis was at hand.

Soon the two lawyers faced one another over the office table, and Blake got to business at once.

"Mr. Pinnock," he said, "I am asked to act for Margaret Donohoe, or Margaret Grant as she claims to be; and I want you to believe that I am seriously telling you what I believe to be the truth, when I say that Miss Grant had better settle this case."

"Why should she pay one penny? What proofs have you? It looks to me, with all respect to you, Mr. Blake, like an ordinary case of blackmail."

"If it were blackmail," said Blake quietly, "do you think that I would be here, giving you particulars of the case? I tell you, man, I am ready now to give you all particulars, and you can soon see whether to advise a settlement or not."

"Fire away, then," said Pinnock. "It will take a lot to convince me, though, and so I tell you."

Blake gave him the particulars gleaned from Peggy. "I have examined and cross-examined and re-cross-examined her, and I can't shake her story."

Pinnock listened with an immovable face, but his mind was working like lightning. As the name of the missionary and Pike's Hotel were mentioned, he remembered that he had seen these very names on the butts of Grant's cheque-books. Getting Blake to excuse him for a moment, he hurried to his room and pulled out a bundle of cheque-butts. The best diary of many a man is found in his cheque-butts. There he saw on the very date mentioned by Blake, cheques drawn to "Self and P.", also one drawn to "Pike accommodation," and one simply to the name of Nettleship for five pounds. Of course it was quite possible that the latter was only a donation to charity, such as old Bully was occasionally very free with; but, taken together, the whole lot made Blake's story look unpleasantly probable. Pinnock whistled to himself as he tied the bundle up again. "Case of settle or be sorry," he said to himself. "I wonder how much will settle it?"

When he faced Blake again, he had pulled the mask of professional stolidity over his features; also he lied boldly.

"I can see nothing to corroborate this story," he said; "but it may be that Miss Grant would rather pay a few pounds than have the unpleasantness of a trial. I will get her in and ask her if you like, but I don't think it will lead to anything."

They were holding their conference in the office. Outside, the station was dozing in the sun. The house dog slept in the yard, and a stray wild pigeon had come down into the quadrangle, and was picking at some grain that was spilt there. From the garden came the shouts of the children and the happy laughter of Mary Grant.

"There she is now," said Pinnock. "Hadn't I better get her to come in and get the thing over?"

He went out, and came back very soon. "Mrs. Gordon and Miss Grant are coming," he said. "She said she would like Mrs. Gordon to be with her."

Before long they came in and sat down. Mary Grant had no idea what she was wanted for. She greeted Blake with a glad smile, and waited to hear what Pinnock had to say. It did not take the lawyer long to put the story before her: but it was some time before she could understand it. Nothing so tragic had ever entered her life before, and she seemed almost stunned.

Mrs. Gordon moved to her side and took her hand.

"It is very terrible for you—for us all, dear," she said. "You must listen to what Mr. Pinnock says, and make up your mind. He can advise you best what to do."

Again Pinnock went through the case. As a full understanding broke in on her, she drew herself up; the look of distress and perplexity left her face, and her eyes were full of scorn and anger.

"Hello, what's coming now?" thought Pinnock. "I hope she says nothing rash."

She tried to speak once or twice, but the words seemed to choke her.

"What do you advise me to do, Mr. Pinnock?" she said, turning to him suddenly.

"I advise you to give me power to act for you in the matter as I think best," said Pinnock, who saw that matters were likely to slip beyond his control. "From what Mr. Blake tells me, I daresay this woman can give you a lot of trouble and annoyance. Whatever you pay her, you won't miss the money. You will save the family here from being turned out; you will avoid scandal; and if there should be any foundation for Mr. Blake's story, it may mean that if you don't settle you lose everything."

From him Mary Grant turned to the old lady.

"Mrs. Gordon," she said, "do you advise me to pay this money?"

"My dear, I don't advise at all. Don't consider us in the matter at all. It is for you to say."

"Then I will pay nothing. It is a cruel, infamous, wicked slander. These poor, ignorant people don't know what they are doing. Sooner than pay one penny in compromise, I will walk off this station a pauper. God will not let such villainy win. Mrs. Gordon, surely you don't think that I ought to blacken my father's and mother's name by paying money to keep this claim quiet?"

Here Pinnock broke in on her speech. "But if they should manage to produce evidence—"

"Let them produce it, and let the judge believe it if he likes. You and I and everybody know that it is a lie; even if they win the case, it is still a lie. I will pay nothing—not one halfpenny. My mother's name is more than all the money in the world, and I will not blacken it by compromises. Mr. Pinnock, the case is to be fought out, and if we lose we shall still know that justice is on our side; but if we pay money—"

Mrs. Gordon took her hand, and lifted it to her lips.

"I think you are quite right, my dear. You put us all to shame for even thinking of it."

"I am very sorry, Mr. Blake," the girl went on, "very sorry indeed that you should have come here on such an errand. You saved my life, and if I could pay you for that I would; but this offer is an insult, and I hope that you will never come here again. Whether I am turned out of the old station or not, I hope that you will never come here again." And with that the two ladies walked out, leaving the lawyers looking at each other.

"I am afraid, Mr. Blake" said Pinnock at last, "that we have lost any hope we might ever have had of settling this case."

But Blake, as he rode homewards, felt that he had lost for ever a much higher hope. He had played for a high stake on two chances. One of them had failed him. There remained only the chance of pulling Peggy's case through; and he swore that if hard work, skill, and utter unscrupulousness could win that case, it should be won.

CHAPTER XXII
A NURSE AND HER ASSISTANT

While they were waiting for the great case to come on a sort of depression seemed to spread itself over the station. The owner was mostly shut up in her room with her thoughts; the old lady was trying to comfort her, and Ellen Harriott, with sorrow always at her heart, went about the household work like an automaton. No wonder that as soon as breakfast was over all the men cleared out to work on the run. But one day it so happened that Carew did not go out with the others. The young Englishman was a poor correspondent, and had promised himself a whole quiet day to be spent in explaining by letter to his people at home the mysterious circumstances under which he had found and lost Patrick Henry Considine. Ellen Harriott found him in the office manfully wrestling with some extra long words, and stopped for a few minutes' talk. She had a liking for the young Englishman, and any talk was better than to be left alone with her thoughts.

"These are bad times for the old station, Mr. Carew," she said. "We don't know what is going to happen next."

Carew was not going to haul down the flag just yet. "I believe everything 'll come all right in the long run, don't you know," he said. "Never give up first hit, you know; see it out—eh, what?"

"I want to get away out of this for a while," she said. "I am run down. I think the bush monotony tells on women. I don't want anyone to fall sick, but I do wish I could get a little nursing to do again—just for a change. I would nurse Red Mick himself."

Is there anything in telepathy? Do coming events sometimes send warnings on ahead? Certain it is that, even as she spoke, a rider on a sweating horse was seen coming at full speed up the flat; he put his horse over the sliprails that led into the house paddock without any hesitation, and came on at a swinging gallop.

"What is this?" said Ellen Harriott, "more trouble? It is only trouble that comes so fast. Why, it is one of Red Mick's nephews!" By this time the rider was up to them; without dismounting he called out Miss! Please, Miss! There's been an accident. My uncle got run agin a tree and he's all smashed in the head. I'm off to the Doctor now; I'll get the Doctor here by to-morrow night, and would you go out and do aught you can for Mick? There's no one out there but old Granny, and she's helpless like. Will you go?"

"Is he much hurt?"

"I'm afraid he's killed, Miss. I found him, He'd been out all night and the side of his head all busted. After a dingo he was—I seen the tracks. Coming back from Gavan Blake's he must 'a' seen the dorg off the track, and the colt he was on was orkard like and must have hit him agen a tree. The colt kem home with the saddle under his belly, and I run the tracks back till I found him. Will you go out, Miss?"

"Yes," said Ellen, "I will go. And you hurry on now, and get the Doctor. Tell the Doctor I've gone out there." Like an arrow from the bow the young fellow sent his big thoroughbred horse across the paddocks, making a bee line over fences and everything for Tarrong, while Ellen Harriott hurried in to pack up a few things.

"Can I help you at all?" said Carew, following her into the house. I'd like to be some use, don't you know; but in this country I seem to be so dashed useless."

"You will be a lot of use if you will come out with me. I shall want someone to drive the trap out, and I may want help with the patient. You are big and strong."

"Yes, and it's about the first time my strength has even been of any use to anybody. I will go and get the trap ready while you dress."

Hurriedly they packed food and blankets into the light buggy, and set off. Miss Harriott knew the tracks well, and the buggy fairly flew along till they came up the flat to Red Mick's. As they drew near the hut a noise of talking and crying came through the open door.

"What's up now?" said Carew. "Crowd of people there."

"No"—Ellen Harriott listened for a second. "No," she said, "he is delirious. That is the old woman crying. Hurry up, Mr. Carew—take the horse out of the buggy and put him in the stable, and then come in as quickly as you can. I may want help."

Leaving Carew to unharness the horse, she went inside. In the inner roomy on a bunk, lay Red Mick. Eye, nose, forehead, and mouth were all one unrecognisable lump, while fragments of bark and splinters still stuck to the skin. In the corner sat the old mother, crying feebly. Disregarding the old woman, Ellen made a swift examination of Mick's injuries, but as soon as he felt her touch on his face he sprang to his feet and struck at her.

Just as he did so, Carew rushed in and threw his arms round the madman. In that grip even Red Mick had no power to move.

"Just hold him quiet," said Ellen, "till I have a look"—and she rapidly ran her fingers over the wound. "Very bad. I think there must be a bit of the skull pressing on the brain. We can't do much till the Doctor comes. I think he will be quiet now. Will you make a fire and boil some water, so that I can clean and dress the wound That will ease him a little. And get the blankets in; we can make up some sort of place on the floor to sleep. One of us will have to watch all night. Cranny, you must go to bed, do you hear? Come and sit by Mick till I put Granny to bed."

By degrees they got things shipshape—put the old woman to bed, and cleaned and dressed Mick's wounds. Then they settled down for the long night in the sick-room. A strange sick-room it was; but many a hospital is less healthy. Through wide cracks between the slabs there came in the cool, fresh air that in itself is worth more than all the medicines in the pharmacopoeia. The patient had sunk into an uneasy slumber when Ellen made her dispositions for the night.

"You go and lie down now," she said, "in the other room, on the sofa. I will call you if I want you. Get all the sleep you can, and in a couple of hours you can take my place. He may talk, but don't let that disturb you. I will call out loud enough if I want you."

"Mind you do," said the Englishman. "I sleep like a blessed top, you know. Sleep anywhere. Well, good-night for the present. He looks a little better since you washed him, doesn't he?"

He threw himself on the couch in the inner room, and before long a titanic snore showed that he had not over-rated his sleeping powers.

Ellen Harriott sat by Red Mick's bedside and thought over the events of the last few weeks. As she thought she half-dozed, but woke with a start to find her patient broad awake again and trying to get at something that was under his bunk. Quietly she drew him back, for his struggles with Carew had left him weak as a child.

He looked at her with crazed eyes.

"The paper," he said, "for the love of God, the paper. I have to take it to Gavan. 'Twill win the case. The paper."

She tried to pacify him, but nothing would do but that she should get the mysterious paper. At last, to humour him, she dived under the bunk and found an iron camp-oven, and in it a single envelope. Just to see what was exciting him she opened the envelope, and found a crumpled piece of paper which she read over to herself. It was the original certificate of the marriage between Patrick Henry Keogh and Margaret Donohoe; if Ellen had only known it, she held in her hand the evidence to sweep away all her friend's troubles. It so happened, however, that it conveyed nothing to her mind. She had heard much about Considine, but not a word about Keogh, and the name "Margaret Donohoe" did not strike her half-asleep mind as referring to Peggy. She put the paper away again in the camp-oven; then, feeling weary, she awoke Carew and lay down on the couch while he watched the patient.

Next morning the Doctor arrived with a trail of Red Mick's relations after him; among them they arranged to take him into Tarrong to be operated on, and Ellen Harriott and Carew drove back to Kuryong feeling as if they had known each other all their lives.

As they drove along she wondered idly which of Red Mick's innumerable relatives the paper referred to, and why Mick was so anxious about it; but by the time they arrived at home the matter passed from her mind, except that she remembered well enough what was written on the odd-looking little scrap.

"I will give you a certificate as a competent wardsman if ever you want one," she said to Carew as he helped her out of the buggy. "I don't know what I'd have done without you."

"You'd have managed somehow, I'll bet," he said, looking at the confident face before him. "Quite a bit of fun, wasn't it? I hope we have a few more excursions together."

And she felt that she rather hoped so, too.

CHAPTER XXIII
HUGH GOES IN SEARCH

Who does not remember the first exciting news of the great Grant v. Grant will case? The leading Q.C.'s. watched eagerly for briefs; juniors who held even the smallest briefs in connection with it patronised their fellows, and explained to them intricate legal dodges which they themselves had thought out and "pumped into" their learned leaders. "Took me a doose of a time to get him to see it, but I think he has got it at last," they used to say. The case looked like lasting for years, for there would be appeals and counter-appeals, references, inquiries and what not; and in getting ready for the first fight the lawyers on each side worked like beavers.

Blake let it be known among the clans that he was going to fight the case for Peggy, and that there was going to be a lawsuit such as the most veteran campaigner of them all had never even dimly imagined—a lawsuit with the happiness of a beautiful woman and the disposal of a vast fortune at stake. Word was carried from selection to selection, across trackless mountain-passes, and over dangerous river crossings, until even Larry, the outermost Donohoe, heard the news in his rocky fastness, miscalled a grazing lease, away in the gullies under the shadows of Black Andrew mountain. By some mysterious means it even reached Briney Doyle, who was camped out near the foothills of Kosciusko, running wild horses into trap-yards. This occupation had taken such hold on him that he had become as wild as the horses he pursued, and it was popularly supposed that the other Doyles had to go out with horses to run him in whenever they wanted him.

Peggy brought in the copy of her marriage certificate, an old and faded piece of paper which ran—"This is to certify that I, Thomas Nettleship, duly ordained clergyman of the Church of England, have this day solemnized a marriage between William Grant, Bachelor, and Margaret Donohoe, Spinster."

The name of Pike's Hotel and the date were nearly illegible, but there the document was; and though it was not the original certificate, it was pretty clear that Peggy could never have invented it. Its production made a great impression. It certainly went far to convince Blake.

He had cross-examined all the witnesses, had checked their accounts by each other, had followed William Grant's career at that time, had got on to the history of the bush missionary; and everything fitted in. Martin Doyle—Black Martin's son Martin—was letter-perfect in his part. Peggy could give the details of the ceremony with unfaltering accuracy fifty times a day if need be, and never contradict herself. So at last he gave up trying to find holes in the case, and determined to go in and win.

On the other side there was trouble in the camp—no witnesses could be found, except Martin Doyle, and he was ready to swear to the wedding. At last it became evident that the only chance of overthrowing Peggy's case was to find Considine; but the earth seemed to have swallowed him up.

The influence of the Chief of Police was brought to bear, and many a weary mile did the troopers of the Outer Back ride in search of the missing man. One of them followed a Considine about two hundred miles across country, and embodied the story of his wanderings in a villainously written report; brief and uncouth as the narrative was, it was in itself an outline picture of bush life. From shearers' hut to artesian borers' camp, from artesian well to the opal-fields, from the opal-fields to a gold-rush, from the gold-rush to a mail-coach stable, he pursued this Considine, only to find that, in the words of the report, "the individual was not the same."

Things looked hopeless for Mary Grant, when help came from an unexpected quarter. A letter written in a rugged, forcible fist, arrived for Charlie Gordon from a young fellow named Redshaw, once a stationhand on Kuryong, who had gone out to the back-country and was rather a celebrity in his way. His father was a pensioner at the old station, and Redshaw junior, who was known as Flash Jack, evidently kept in touch with things at Kuryong. He wrote

> Dear Sir,
>
> I hear from Gannon the trooper that you want to find Keogh. When he left the coach that time, he went back to the station and got his horses, and cleared out, and he is now hiding in Reeves's buffalo camp at the back of Port Faraway. If I hear any more will let you know.
>
> J. REDSHAW, alas 'Flash Jack.'"

"What's all this?" said Pinnock, when Charlie and Carew brought him the letter. "Who is J. Redshaw, and why does he sign "alas Flash Jack?"

"He means *Alias*, don't you see? *Alias* Flash Jack. He is a man we used to have on the station, and his father used to work for us—I expect he wants to do us a good turn."

"It will be a good turn in earnest, if he puts you in the way of finding Considine," said the lawyer. "You will have to send Hugh up. The old man knows you and Carew, and if he saw you coming he would take to the woods, as the Yankees say. Even when you do get him the case isn't over, because the jury will side with Peggy. They'll sympathise with her efforts to prove herself an honest woman. It isn't marrying too much that will get her into trouble—it's the other thing. But we have the date and place of her alleged marriage with William Grant; and if this old Considine can prove, by documents, mind you, not by his own simple word—because it's a hundred to one the jury wouldn't believe him—I say, if he can prove that she married him on that very day and at that very place, then she's beaten. No one on earth could swallow the story of her marrying two different people on the same day."

"Hugh can go," said Charlie. "He'll have to do his best this time. It all depends on getting hold of this Considine, eh? Well, Hugh 'll have to get him. If he fails he needn't show his face amongst us any more."

Mary Grant was called in and told the great news, and then Pinnock started out to find Hugh. But before the lawyer could see him, Mary met him in the garden.

Hugh did not see that he could be of any use in the case, and wanted to be quit of Kuryong for good. Seeing Mary day after day, he had become more and more miserable as the days went by. He determined at last to go away altogether, and, when once he had made up his mind, only waited for a chance to tell her that he was going. The chance came as she left the office after consulting with Pinnock.

"Miss Grant," he said, "if you don't mind, I think I will resign my management of this station. I will make a start for myself or get a job somewhere else. You will easily get someone to take my place."

She looked at him keenly for a while.

"I didn't expect this of you," she said, bitterly. "The rats leave the sinking ship. Is that it?"

His face flushed a dull red. "You know better than that," he said. "I would stop if I could be of any use, but what is there I can do?"

"Why do you want to leave?"

"I want to get away from here—I want to get out of the hills for awhile."

Mary knew, as well as if he had told her, that what he wanted was to go where he could forget her and see whether absence would break the chain; and triumph lit up her eyes, for it was pleasant even in the midst of her troubles to know that he still cared. Then she came to a swift decision.

"Will you do something for me away from the hills, then?" she said.

"Where?"

"Up North. I want some one to find that man Considine that your brother and Mr. Carew met. You know how important it is to me. Will you do it for me?"

Hugh would have jumped at the chance to risk his life for her lightest wish.

"I will go anywhere and do my best to find anyone you want," he said; "When do you want me to start?"

"See Mr. Pinnock and your brother about that. They will tell you all about it; and if you do manage to find this man, why, you can talk about leaving after that if you want to. Will you go for me?"

"Yes. I will go, Miss Grant; and I will never come back till I find this man—if he is alive."

She laid her hand on his arm.

"I know you will do all you can," she said, "but in any case, whether you find him or not—come back again!"

CHAPTER XXIV
THE SECOND SEARCH FOR CONSIDINE

Before leaving Hugh was fully instructed what to do if he compassed the second finding of Considine. He was to travel under another name, for fear that his own would get about, and cause the fugitive to make another hurried disappearance.

He took a subpœna to serve on the old man as a last resource.

Charlie was emphatic. "Go up and get hold of the old vagrant, and find out all about it. Don't make a mess of it, whatever you do. Remember the old lady, and Miss Grant, and the youngsters, and all of us depend on you in this business. Don't come back beaten. Don't let anything stop you. Get him drunk or get him sober—friendly or fighting—but get the truth, and get the proofs of it. Choke it out of the old hound somehow."

Hugh said that he would, and departed, weighed down by responsibility, to execute his difficult mission. He had to go into an untravelled country to get the truth out of a man who did not want to tell it; and the time allowed was short, as the case could not be postponed much longer.

He travelled by sea to Port Faraway, a tropical sweltering township by the Northern seas of Australia, and when he reached it felt like one of the heroes in Tennyson's Lotus Eaters—he had come "into a land wherein it seemed always afternoon."

Reeves, the buffalo shooter, was a well-known man, but to find his camp was another matter. No one seemed to have energy enough to take much interest in the quest.

Hugh interviewed a leading citizen at the hotel, and got very little satisfaction. He said, "I want to get out to Reeves's camp. Do you know where it is, and how one gets there?"

"Well," said the leading citizen, putting his feet up on the arms of his long chair and gasping for air, "Le's see! Reeves's camp—ah! Where is he camped now?"

"I don't know," said Hugh. "I wish I did. That's what I want to find out."

"Hopkins'd know. Hopkins, the storekeeper. He sends out the supplies. Did you ask him?"

"No," said Hugh. "I didn't. I'll go and ask him now."

"Too hot to bustle round now," said the leading citizen, lighting his pipe. "What'll you have to drink? Have some square; it's the best drink here."

Hugh thought it well to fall in with the customs of the inhabitants, so he had a stiff gin-and-water at nine in the morning, a thing he had never done, or even seen done, in his life before. Then he went over in the blazing sunlight to the storekeeper, and asked whether he knew where Reeves' camp was.

"That I don't," said the storekeeper. "I send out what they want by a Malay who sails a one-masted craft round the coast, and goes up the river to their camp, and brings the hides back. They send a blackfellow to let me know when they want any stuff, and where to send it."

"Perhaps I could go out with the next lot of stuff," said Hugh. "When will they want it, do you think?"

"Well, they mightn't want any more. They might go on now till the wet season, and then they'll come in."

"When is the wet season, then?"

"Oh, a couple of months, likely. Perhaps three months. Perhaps there won't be none at all to speak of. What'll you have?"

"Oh, I have just had a drink, thanks. Fact is, I'm a bit anxious to get out to this camp. It's a bit important. You don't know where they are for certain?"

"Lord knows! Anywhere! Might be on one river, might be on another. They'll come in in the wet season. Better have a drink, anyhow. You must have something. What'll it be—square? Beer? Can't stand beer in this climate, myself."

"Oh, well," said Hugh desperately, "I'll have another square. Make it a light one. Do you think I can get anyone who knows where they are camped to go out with me?"

"Tommy Prince'd know, I expect. He was out in that country before. But he's gone with a bullock-team, drawing quartz to the new battery at the Oriental. At least I saw him start out three weeks ago. Said he was in a hurry, too, as the battery couldn't start until he got the quartz hauled."

"Perhaps he didn't start," said Hugh; "perhaps he put it off till after the wet season?"

"Well," said the storekeeper, meditatively, "he might, but I don't think he would. There's no one else, that I know of, can find them for you. Lord knows where they are. They camp in one place till the buffalo are all shot, and then they shift to new ground. Perhaps ten miles, perhaps thirty. Have another drink? What'll you have?"

"No, not any more, thanks. About this Tommy Prince, now; if I can find him he might tell me where to go. Where can I find him?"

"Down at the Margaret is where he camps, but I think he's gone to the Oriental by this time—sure to be. That's about forty miles down past the Margaret. There was a fellow came in from the Margaret for supplies, and he'll be going back to-morrow—if he can find his pack-horses."

"And supposing he can't?"

"Well, then, he'll go out next week, I expect, unless he gets on the drink. He's a terrible chap to drink."

"And if he starts to drink, when will he go?"

"Lord knows. They'll have to send in after him. His mates'll be pretty near starved by now, anyhow. He's been in town, foolin' round that girl at the Royal this three weeks. He'll give you a lift out to the Margaret—that's forty miles."

"What is there out at the Margaret when I get there? Is it a town, or a station, or a mine? What is it?"

"Oh, it's not so bad. There's a store there, and a few mines scattered about. Mostly Chinese mines. The storekeeper there's a great soaker, nearly always on the drink. Name's Sampson. He'll tell you where to find Tommy Prince. Prince and his mates have a claim twelve miles out from there, and if Tommy ain't gone to the Oriental, he might go down with you."

"Supposing Tommy's at his claim, twelve miles out," said Hugh, "how can I get out?"

"I dunno," said the storekeeper, who was getting tired of talking so long without a drink. "I dunno how you'll get out there. Better have a drink—what'll you have?"

Hugh walked out of the store in despair. He found himself engaged in what appeared to be an endless chase after a phantom Considine, and the difficulties in his way semed insuperable. Yet how could he go back and tell them all at home that he had failed? What would they think of him? The thought made him miserable; and he determined, if he failed, never to go back to the old station at all.

So he returned to his hotel, packed his valise, and set out to look for the pack-horse man. He found him fairly sober; soon bargained to be allowed to ride one of the horses, and in due course was deposited at the Margaret—a city consisting of one galvanised-iron building, apparently unoccupied. His friend dismounted and had a drink with him out of his flask. They kicked at the door unavailingly; then his mate went on into the indefinite, leaving him face to face with general desolation.

The Margaret store was the only feature in the landscape—a small building with a heap of empty bottles in the immediate foreground, and all round it the grim bush, a vista of weird twisted trees and dull grey earth with scanty grass. At the back were a well, a windlass, and a trough for water, round which about a hundred goats were encamped. Hugh sat and smoked, and looked at the prospect. By-and-by out of the bush came two men, a Chinaman and a white man. The Chinaman was like all Chinamen; the white man was a fiery, red-faced, red-bearded, red-nosed little fellow. The Chinee was dragging a goat along by the horns, the goat hanging back and protesting loudly in semi-human screams; every now and again a black mongrel dog would make sudden fiendish dashes at the captive, and fasten its teeth in its neck. This made it bellow louder; but the Chinaman, with the impassibility of his race, dragged goat, dog, and all along, without the slightest show of interest.

The white man trudged ahead, staring fixedly in front; when they reached the store he stared at Hugh as if he were the Bunyip, but said no word. Then he unlocked the door, went in, and came out with a large knife, with which he proceeded to murder the goat scientifically. The Chinee meanwhile bailed up the rest of the animals, and caught and milked a couple of "nannies," while a patriarchal old "billy" walked fragrantly round the yard, uttering hoarse "buukhs" of defiance.

It was a truly pastoral scene, but Hugh took little interest in it. He was engrossed with the task of getting out to the buffalo camp, finding Considine, and making him come forward and save the family. He approached the white, or rather red man, who cocked a suspicious eye at him, and went on tearing the hide off the goat. Hugh noticed that his hand trembled a good deal, and that a sort of foam gathered on his lips as he worked.

"Good day," said Hugh.

The man glared at him, but said nothing.

"My name is Lambton," said Hugh. "I want to go out to the buffalo camp. I want to find Tommy Prince, to see if he can go out with me. Do you know where he is?"

The man put the blade of the butcher's knife between his teeth, and stared again at Hugh, apparently having some difficulty in focussing him. Then his lips moved, and he was evidently trying to frame speech. He said, "Boo, Boo, Boo," for a few seconds; then he pulled himself together, and said,

"Wha' you want?"

"I want to get to the buffalo camp," said Hugh. "You know Reeves's camp."

Here a twig fell to the ground just behind the man; he gave one blood-curdling yell, dropped the knife, and rushed past Hugh, screaming out, "Save me! Save me! They're after me! Look at 'em; look at 'em!" His hair stood perfectly erect with fright, and, as he ran, he glanced over his shoulder with frightened eyes. He didn't get far. In his panic he ran straight towards the well, banged his head against the windlass, and went thundering down the twenty or thirty feet of shaft souse into the water at the bottom, where he splashed and shrieked like a fiend, the noise reverberating up the long shaft.

Hugh and the Chinaman ran to the well-top, Hugh cursing under his breath. Every possible obstacle that could arise had arisen to block his journey; every man that could have helped him was away, or dead, or otherwise missing; and now, to crown all, after getting thus far, he had apparently struck a prize lunatic, and would have to stay in that awful desolation, perhaps for a week, with him and a Chinaman. Perhaps he would have to give evidence on the lunatic's dead body, and even be accused of causing his death. All these thoughts flashed through his mind as he ran to the well-head. From the noise he made the man was evidently not dead yet, and, looking down, he saw his eyes glaring up as he splashed in the water.

"What's up with him?" roared Hugh to the Chinaman.

"Him, dlink, dlink—all-a-time dlink, him catchee hollows."

They had started to lower the bucket, when suddenly the yells ceased, a loud bubbling was heard, and looking down they saw only a dim, round object above the water. Without an instant's delay Hugh put his foot in the bucket and signed to the Chinee to lower him. Swiftly and silently he descended the well, jumped out of the bucket, and grabbed the floating body of the drunkard with one hand, holding on to the rope with the other. The man had collapsed, and was as limp as a rag. Hugh made the rope fast under his armpits, and gave the old mining cry, "On top there, haul away."

Heavily the windlass creaked. Mightily the Chinee strained. The unconscious figure was drawn out of the water and up the shaft, inch by inch. The weight of a man in wet clothes is considerably more than that of a bucket of water, and it seemed a certainty that either the old windlass would break or the Chinaman's arms give out. Slowly, slowly, the limp wet figure ascended the shaft, while Hugh supported himself in the water, by gripping the logs at the side of the well, praying that the tackle would hold. The creaking of the windlass ceased, and the ascending body stopped — evidently the Chinee was pausing to get his breath.

"Go on!" screamed Hugh. "Keep at it, John! Don't let it beat you! Wind away!"

Faintly came the gasped reply, "No can! No more can do!"

He lowered himself in the water as far as he could, to deaden the blow in case of the fellow falling back on him, and screamed encouragement, threats, and promises up the well. Suddenly from above came a new voice altogether, a white man's voice.

"Right oh, boss! We've got him."

The windlass recommenced its creaking, and the figure at the end of the rope continued its slow, upward journey. Hugh saw the body hauled slowly to the top and grabbed by a strong hand; then it disappeared, and the sunlight once more streamed, uninterrupted, down the shaft. The bucket came down again, and Hugh clutched it and yelled out, "Haul away!" He could hear the men grunting above as they turned the handle.

When he had been hauled about fifteen feet there was a crack; the old windlass had collapsed, and he went souse, feet first, into the water. He sank till he touched the bottom, then rose gasping to the surface. A head appeared, framed in the circle of the well, and a slow, drawling colonial voice said:

"Gord! boss, are you hurt? The windlass is broke."

"No, I'm not hurt. Can't you fix that windlass?" roared Hugh.

"No!" came the answer sepulchrally down the well. "She's cooked."

"Well, hold on," said Hugh. "I believe I can get up." He braced his feet against one side of the well, and his shoulders against the other, and so, working them alternately, he raised himself inch by inch. It is a feat that requires a good man to perform, and the strain was very great. Grimly he kept at it, and drew nearer and nearer to the top. Then, at last, a hand seized him; half-sick with over-exertion, he struggled out and fell gasping to the ground. For a minute or two the universe was turning round with him. The

Chinee and the strange white man moved in a kind of flicker, unreal as the figures in a cinematograph. Then all was blank for a while.

When he came to, he was lying by the well with a bag under his head, and the strange white man was trying to pour some spirits down his throat.

"I'm—all right—thanks!" gasped Hugh.

"By Gord, Mister, it's lucky I happened to come along," said the stranger. "You an' Sampson'd ha' both been drownded. That Chow couldn't haul him up. Dead beat the Chow was when I came. I jis' come ridin' up, thinkin' to get a few pound of onions to take out to the camp, and I see the Chow a-haulin' and a-haulin' at that windlass like as if he was tryin' to pull the bottom out of the well. I rides up and sings out "What ho! Chaney, what yer got?" And he says, "Ketch hold," he says, and that was all he could say; he was fair beat. And then I heard you singing out, and I says to meself, "Is the whole popperlation of the Northern Territory down this here well? How many more is there, Chancy?" I says. And then bung goes the old windlass, and lucky it ketched in the top of the well; if it had fell down on the top of you, it'd ha' stiffened you all right. And how you got up that well beats me. By Cripes, it does."

"How's the—man that—was down with me?" said Hugh slowly.

"What, Sampson? 'E's all right. Couldn't kill'm with a meat-axe. He must ha' swallowed very near all the water in that well. Me an' the Chow emptied very near two buckets out of him. He's dead to the world jes' now. How do you feel, boss?"

"I'll be all right in a minute," said Hugh. "What's your name?"

"I'm Tommy Prince," said the stranger. "I jist kem in from my camp to-day for them onions."

Hugh drew a long breath. The luck had turned at last.

CHAPTER XXV
IN THE BUFFALO CAMP

"You're just the man I was looking for," said Hugh, taking in the stranger with his eyes. "I want to get out to Reeves's buffalo camp, and I hear you're the only man who knows that country at all. Can you get time to come down with me? I'll make it worth your while."

He waited for the reply with a beating heart. If this man failed him he saw nothing for it but to go back. The stranger lit his pipe with the leisurely movements of a man who had never been in a real hurry in his life.

Then he spoke slowly.

"Well, it's this way, boss, you see. I'm just startin' off in no end of a hurry to go and take a team of bullocks to the Oriental to draw quartz."

"Can't you put it off for a while?" said Hugh. "It's getting near the wet season."

"Well, I'd like to go with you, boss, but I couldn't chuck 'em over—not rightly I couldn't." He stroked his beard and relapsed into thought.

"Let's go in and get a drink," said Hugh. "I suppose there is some square-face inside."

The square-face settled it. They had one drink, and the stranger began to think less of the needs of the Oriental. They had another, and he said he didn't suppose it'd matter much if the Oriental had to wait a bit for their stone, and the bullocks were all over the bush and very poor, and by the time he got them together the wet season would be on. They had a third, and he said that the Oriental had been hanging on for six months, and it wouldn't hurt it to hang on for seven, and he wouldn't see a man like Hugh stuck.

So the shareholders in that valuable concern, the Oriental Mine, were kept in pleasing suspense for some months longer, while the mine-manager (whose salary was going on all the time) did nothing but smoke, and write reports to the effect that "a very valuable body of stone was at grass, awaiting cartage to the battery, when a splendid crushing was a certainty."

Meanwhile Tommy Prince was gaily journeying with Hugh down to the buffalo camp.

Prince, a typical moleskin-trousered, cotton-shirted, cabbage-tree-hatted bushman, soon fixed up all details. He annexed the horses belonging to the store, sagely remarking that, as Hugh had saved their owner's life, he could afford to let him have a few horses. He also helped himself to pack-saddles, camping gear, supplies, and all sorts of odds and ends—not forgetting a couple of gallons of rum, mosquito-nets made of cheese cloth, blankets, and a rifle and cartridges. They fitted out the expedition in fine style, while unconscious Sampson slept the sleep of the half-drowned. The placid Chinese cook fried great lumps of goat for them to eat, heedless of all things except his opium-pipe, to which he had recourse in the evening, the curious dreamy odour of the opium blending strangely with the aromatic scent of the bush.

At daylight they started, and for three days rode through the wilderness, camping out at night, while the horses with bells and hobbles grazed round the camp. Tommy Prince steered a course by instinct, guided as unerringly as the Israelites by their pillar of fire.

By miles of trackless, worthless wilderness, by rolling open plains, by rocky ranges and stony passes, they pushed out and ever further out, till at last, one day, Tommy said, "They ought to be hereabouts, some place." So saying, he dropped a lighted match into a big patch of grass, and in a few seconds a line of fire half a mile wide was roaring across the plain; above it rose smoke as of a burning city.

"They'll see that," said Tommy, "without the buff'loes have got 'em." So they camped for the day under a huge banyan-fig tree and awaited developments. About evening, away on the horizon, there arose an answering cloud of smoke, connecting earth and sky, like a waterspout.

"That's them," said Tommy. They climbed once more into their saddles, and set out. Just as the sun was setting, they saw a singular procession coming towards them. In front rode two small, wiry, hard-featured, inexpressibly dirty men on big well-formed horses. They wore dungaree trousers, which had once been blue, but were now begrimed and bloodstained to a dull neutral colour. Their shirts—once coloured, but now nearly black—were worn outside the trousers, like a countryman's smock frock, and were drawn in at the waist by broad leathern belts full of cartridges. Their faces were half-hidden by stubbly beards, and their bright alert eyes looked out from under the brims of two as dilapidated felt hats as ever graced head of man. Each carried a carbine between thigh and saddle. These were the buffalo shooters.

Behind them rode an elderly, grizzled man, whom Hugh had no difficulty in recognising as Keogh, or Considine. Following him were some seven or eight packhorses, all heavily laden with hides. And behind the packhorses rode three or four naked blacks and a Chinaman.

Hugh's guide at once made himself welcome in his happy-go-lucky style. He introduced Hugh as Mr. Lambton, from New South Wales. The buffalo shooters made him welcome after the fashion of their kind; but Considine was obviously uneasy, and avoided him, riding with Tommy Prince for a while, and evidently trying to find out what Hugh had come for.

That night, when they got to the buffalo shooters' camp, Hugh opened fire on Considine. The veteran was in a cheerful mood after his meal, and Hugh wanted to start diplomatically, thinking he might persuade him. If that failed he would give him the summons; but he would start with the *suaviter in modo*. When it came to the point, however, he forgot his diplomacy, and plunged straight into trouble.

"I'll tell you what I've come up here for, Considine," he said. "My name's Hugh Gordon, and I want to find out something about your marriage with Peggy Donohoe."

"Well, if that's what you come for, Mister," said the veteran, pulling a firestick out of the fire, and slowly lighting his pipe, "if that's what you come for"—puff, puff, puff—"you've come on a wild goose chase. I never knew no Peggy Donohoe in my life. My wife"—puff—"was a small, dark woman, named Smith."

"I thought you told my brother that you married Peggy Donohoe."

"So I might have told him," assented the veteran. "Quite likely I did, but I must ha' made a mistake. A man might easy make a mistake over a thing like that. What odds is it to you who I married, anyhow?"

"What odds? Why look here, Considine, it means that my old mother will be turned out of her home. That's some odds to me, isn't it?"

"Yairs, that's right enough, Mister," said the courteous Considine; "it's lots of odds to you, but what I ask you is—what odds is it to me? Why should I go and saddle myself with a she-devil just when I'm coming into a bit of money? I'd walk miles to do her a bad turn."

"Well, if you want to do her a bad turn, come down and block her getting Mr. Grant's estate."

"Yes, an' put her on to meself What next? I tell you, Mister, straight, I wouldn't have that woman tied to me for all the money in China. That English bloke said there was a big fortune for me in England. Well, if I have to take Peggy Donohoe with it, it can stay. I'll live here with the blacks and the buffalo shooters, and I'll get my livin' for meself, same as I got it all my life; but take on Peggy again I will not. Now, that's Domino—that's the dead finish. I won't go with you, and I won't give you no information. And I'm sorry too, 'cause you seem a good sort of a young feller—but I won't do anything that'll mix me up with Peggy any more."

Hugh ground his teeth with mortification. Then he played his next card.

"There's a man they call Flash Jack—do you know him?"

"Perhaps I do, and perhaps I don't," said the sage in a surly tone.

"Well, he told me to ask you to help us. He said to tell you that he particularly wanted you to give evidence if you can."

"Want'll be his master, then," snarled the old man.

"He said he would put the police on to a job about some cattle at Crossroads," said Hugh.

The rage fairly flashed out of Considine's eyes.

"He said that, did he?" he yelled. "The rotten informer! Well, you tell Flash Jack from me that where he can put me away for one thing I can put him away for half-a-dozen; and if I go into gaol for a five-stretch he goes in for ten. I ain't afraid of Flash Jack, nor you either. See that, now!"

Hugh felt that his mission had failed. He pulled out the summons as a last resource, and passed it to the old man.

"What's this?" he said.

"Summons to give evidence," said Hugh.

"Victoria by the Grace of God," read the old man, by the flickering firelight. "Victoria by the Grace of God, eh? Well, see here," he continued, solemnly putting the summons in the fire and watching it blaze, "if Victoria by the Grace of God wants me, she can send for me—send a coach and six for Patrick Henry Considine, late Patrick Henry Keogh! And then I mightn't go! There'll be only one thing make me go where I don't want to go, and that's a policeman at each elbow and another shovin' behind. I'd sooner do a five-stretch than take Peggy back again. And that's the beginning and the end and the middle of it. And now I'll wish you good night."

CHAPTER XXVI
THE SAVING OF CONSIDINE

At grey dawn all the camp was astir. Hugh looked from under his mosquito-net, and saw old Considine over the fire, earnestly frying a large hunk of buffalo meat. He was without a trouble in the world as he turned the hissing steak in the pan. Two black gins in brief garments—a loin cloth and a villainously dirty pyjama-jacket each—were sitting near him, languidly killing the mosquitoes which settled on their bare legs. These were Maggie and Lucy, but they had degenerated with their surroundings. Tommy Prince was oiling a carbine, and one of the shooters was washing his face at a basin formed by scratching a small hole in the ground and pressing a square of canvas into the depression.

The Chinese skinner was sitting on a log, rubbing a huge butcher's knife on a sharpening stone. Away up the plain the horses, about thirty or forty in number, were slowly trooping into camp, hunted by a couple of blackfellows, naked except for little grass armlets worn above the elbow, and sticks stuck through their noses. When the horses reached the camp they formed a squadron under the shade of some trees, and pushed and shoved and circled about, trying to keep the flies off themselves and each other.

Hugh walked over to Tommy Prince at his rifle-oiling, and watched him for a while. That worthy, who was evidently a true sportsman at heart, was liberally baptising with Rangoon oil an old and much rusted Martini carbine, whose ejector refused to work. Every now and then, when he thought he had got it ship-shape, Tommy would put in a fresh cartridge, hold the carbine tightly to his shoulder, shut his eyes, and fire it into space. The rusty old weapon kicked frightfully, after each discharge the ejector jammed, and Tommy ruefully poked the exploded cartridge out with a rod and poured on more oil.

"Blast the carbine!" said Tommy. "It kicks upwards like; it's kicking my nose all skewwhiff."

"Don't put it to your shoulder, you fool," said one of the shooters; "it'll kick your head off. Hold it out in one hand."

"Then it'll kick my arm off," said Tommy.

"No, it won't; you won t feel it at all," said the shooter. "Your arm will give to the recoil. Blaze away!"

"What are you up to with the carbine?" said Hugh.

"I'm going to have a blaze at some of these 'ere buff'loes," said Tommy gaily. "Bill's lent me a horse. They's got a rifle for you, and one for the old man. "We'll give them buff'loes hell to-day. Five rifles—they'll think the French is after them." "Well, but I want to get back," said Hugh. "We mustn't waste any time. What about the store-keeper's horses?"

"Ho! it'd never do to take them straight back again," said Tommy. "Never do. They must have a spell. Besides, what's the hurry?"

And Hugh, recognising that for all the good he could do he might just as well not hurry back again, resigned himself to the inevitable, picked up his bridle, went into the shuffling herd of horses, and caught the one pointed out to him. It was a big, raw-boned, ragged-hipped bay, a horse that would have been a gentleman under any other conditions, but from long buffalo-hunting had become a careless-going, loose-jointed ruffian, taking his life in his hands every day. He bit savagely at Hugh as he saddled him, and altogether proclaimed himself devoid of self-respect and the finer instincts.

Breakfast was despatched almost in silence. The shooters knew vaguely that Hugh's visit was in some way connected with Considine, and that Considine had refused to do what Hugh wanted. But the hospitality of the buffalo camp is as the hospitality of the Arabs of old—the stranger is made welcome whatever his business, and may come and go unquestioned.

Hugh had little desire to talk on the subject of his visit, and Considine maintained a dogged silence. Tommy Prince alone chatted away affably between large mouthfuls of buffalo beef, damper, and tea, airing his views on all subjects, but principally on the fair sex. Meanwhile the blacks were catching the pack-horses, and sharpening their skinning knives. The two horses used by the shooters were brought over to the camp fire and given a small feed each of much-prized maize and oats and bran, that had been brought round in the lugger from Port Faraway with the camp supplies, landed on the river-bank twelve miles off, and fetched in on pack-horses.

"A little more beef, Mister? No? Well, all aboard for the Buffalo Brigade! That's your rifle by the tree. Put this cartridge-belt on and buckle it real tight; if you leave it loose, when you start to gallop it will shake up and down, and shake the soul out of you. Come, Paddy, what are you riding?"

"I'm going to ride the boco [1] ."

[1] One-eyed horse.

"I wouldn't if I was you. He's all right to race up to a buffalo, but that blind eye of his'll fetch him to grief some day. Ride the old grey."

"No fear," said the old man obstinately, "the boco's one eye's worth any horse's two. Me an' the boco will be near the lead when the whips are crackin', take it from me."

"Come along, then!"

Hugh clambered on to his raw-boned steed, known as "Close Up," because he would go so close to the buffaloes, and the procession started. The five white men rode ahead, all smoking with great enjoyment. Hugh was beside one of the shooters, and opened conference with him.

"I've heard a lot about this business," said Hugh, "but never hoped to see it. What are these Australian buffaloes? I thought they were just humped cattle like those little Brahmin cattle."

"People reckon they're the Indian buffalo," said the bushman. "They were fetched here about fifty years ago from Java—just a few pair, and they were let go and went wild, and now they're all over the face of the earth about here. We've shot six hundred of 'em—just the two rifles—in six months. It's not play, I tell you, to shoot and skin six hundred and cure their hides in that time. We'll get a thousand this season."

"Good Lord," said Hugh. "Won't they be shot out?"

"Not they. There's about eight thousand of 'em shot every year for their hides, and it's just like the ordinary increase of a big cattle station. They're all over these plains, and for miles and miles away down the coast, and in the jungles there's thousands of 'em. There's jungles here that are a hundred miles round, and no animal but a buffalo will go into 'em. The blacks say that inside them there's big patches of clear plain, with grass and water, where there's buffaloes as thick as bees; but you can't get at 'em."

"How do you shoot 'em?" said Hugh.

"Race right up alongside 'em, and put the carbine out with one hand, and shoot downwards into the loin. That's the only way to drop 'em. You can shoot bullets into 'em by the hatful everywhere else, and they just turn and charge; and while you are dodging round, first you huntin' the buffalo, and then the buffalo huntin' you, the rest of the mob are out of sight. You must go right up alongside, close enough to touch 'em with the barrel, and fire down—so." He illustrated with the carbine as he spoke. "And whatever you do, don't pull your horse about; he knows the game, if you don't. Never stop your horse near a wounded buffalo, either. They make a rush as sudden as lightnin'. They look clumsy and big; but, my oath, a wounded one can hop along something wonderful! They'll surprise you for pace any time; but most of all when they're wounded."

"Do they always come at you when they're wounded?" said Hugh.

"Always," said the shooter, "and very often when they're not wounded they'll turn and charge if you've run 'em a long way. You want to look out, I tell you. They'll wheel very sudden, and if they ketch your horse they'll grind him into pulp. Ben, my mate here, had a horse killed under him last week—horse we gave five and twenty quid for, and that's a long shot for a buffalo horse. I believe in Injia they shoot 'em off elephants, but that's 'cause they won't come out in the open like they do here. There's hundreds of toffs in England and Injia'd give their ears for a day after these, you know. Hello! Look! See there!"

Far away out on the plain Hugh saw fifteen or twenty bluish-grey mounds in a line rising above the grass; it was a herd of buffalo feeding. The animals never lifted their heads, and were curiously like a lot of railway trucks covered with grey tarpaulin. It was impossible to tell which was head and which was tail. A short halt was made while girths were tightened, cartridges slipped into place, and hats jammed on; they all mounted and rode slowly towards the herd, which was at least half a mile off, and still feeding steadily. Everyone kept his horse in hand, ready for a dash the moment the mob lifted their heads.

"How fast will they go?" whispered Hugh to the nearest shooter.

"Fast as blazes. You've no idea how fast they are. They're the biggest take-in there is. When they lift their heads they'll stare for half a minute, and then they'll run. The moment they start, off you go. Watch 'em! There's one sees us! Keep steady yet—don't rush till they start."

One of the blue mounds lifted a huge black-muzzled head, decorated with an enormous pair of sickle-shaped horns that stretched right back to the shoulders. He stared with great sullen eyes and trotted a few paces towards them; one after another, the rest lifted their heads and stared too. Closer drew the horsemen at their steady, silent jog, the horses pricking their ears and getting on their toes as race-horses do at the start of a race.

"Be ready," said the shooter. "Now!"

The mob, with one impulse, wheeled, and set off at a heavy lumbering gallop, and the horses dashed in full gallop after them. It was a ride worth a year of a man's life. Every man sat down to his work like a jockey finishing a race, and the big stock horses went through the long grass like hawks swooping down on a flock of pigeons. The men carried their carbines loaded, holding them straight up over the shoulder so as to lessen the jerking of the wrist caused by the gallop.

The surface of the plain was level enough, but frightfully bad going; the sun had baked the black soil till great gaping cracks, a couple of feet wide and ten feet deep, were opened in the ground. The buffaloes had wallowed in the wet season and made round well-like holes that were now hard, dry pitfalls. Here and there a treacherous, slimy watercourse wound its slinking way along, making a bog in which a horse would sink to his shoulders; and over all these traps and pitfalls the long waving jungle-grass drew a veil. Every now and then belts of small bamboo were crossed, into which the horses dashed blindly, forcing their way through by their weight. When they started the buffaloes had a lead of a quarter of a mile, and judging by their slogging, laboured gallop, it looked as though the horses would run into them in half a mile; but on that ground the buffaloes could go nearly as fast as the horses, and it was only after a mile and a quarter of hard riding that they closed in on the mob, which at once split into several detachments. A magnificent old bull, whose horns measured ten feet from tip to tip, dashed away to the right with six or seven cows lumbering after him. Hugh and one of the shooters followed this lot. Another mob went away to the left, pursued by the other shooter and Considine; while one old cow, having had enough running, suddenly wheeled in her tracks, and charged straight at Tommy Prince, whose horse at once whipped round and carried his rider, with the old cow at his tail, into a clump of bamboos. Hugh followed his mate as hard as he could, both horses feeling the pace, and pecking and blundering every now and again in the broken ground. Once Hugh saw a buffalo-wallow suddenly appear right under his horse's nose, and half-flinched, expecting a certain fall; but old "Close Up" strode over it, apparently having a leg to spare for emergencies of the sort.

Just ahead of him the shooter, sitting down in his saddle, lifted his horse with a drive of the spurs, and came right alongside the hindmost animal, a fat blue cow, which at once swerved at right angles; but the horse followed her every movement, and drew up till horse and buffalo were racing side by side. Then without fuss or hurry, up went the elbow of the rider and bang! the buffalo fell as if paralysed, shot through the lions. The horse swung away from the falling animal as it crashed to the ground; and the shooter, still going at full gallop, methodically ejected the used cartridge and put in another without losing his place at the tail of the flying mob. The noise of the carbine made the mob divide, and Hugh found himself going full speed after three that came his way. Wild with excitement, he drove Close Up after the nearest, and made ready to fire at the right moment. The long gallop had winded him; his arm was almost numbed with the strain of carrying the carbine, which now seemed to weigh a ton.

Close Up, true to his name, made a dash at the nearest buffalo, and got close enough in all conscience; but what with the jerking to and fro of the gallop, and the rolling gait and sudden swerves of the buffalo, and the occasional blunderings of the horse in broken ground, Hugh never seemed to have the carbine pointed right. Close Up, finding it did not go off when he expected, began to slacken pace and gallop in an undecided way. It sounds easy enough to gallop up to an animal which you can beat for pace, but anyone who has ever tried to lay a whip on the back of a bullock knows it is not so easy as it looks to get more than one or two clips home. Hugh found the buffalo holding its own for pace, and every time he drew up it dodged before he could make sure of hitting the loin. Cover seemed to be getting very near. At last he leaned out as far as he could, held the rifle in one hand, and took a "speculator" at the flying buffalo. He hit it somewhere, but hadn't time to see where; for, with a snort like a grampus, the beast wheeled in its tracks and charged so suddenly that old Close Up only just dodged it by a yard or two. It rushed him for a couple of hundred yards, and then stopped. Hugh managed to eject the cartridge and load, and then cantered after the animal, which had started again at a sullen trot, with the blood pouring from its flank. As he galloped up to administer the "coup de grace," meaning to make no mistake about hitting the loin this time, the buffalo suddenly wheeled and charged him again, and Close Up executed another hurried retreat. For a while they took it up and down—first buffalo hunting man, then man hunting buffalo—while Hugh fired whenever he had the chance, without seeming to discompose the brute at all. At last a lucky shot struck some vital spot inside; the beast stopped, staggered, and fell dead without a sound. Hugh looked round. He was alone; his mate was just visible far away over the plain, still following at full speed a blue mound that struggled doggedly on towards the timber. The grey horse drew up to his quarry, the man leant forward, there was a sudden spurt of white smoke, and the animal fell as if struck by lightning. It was very pretty to watch, and looked as simple as shelling peas. The shooter rode over to Hugh, and congratulated him on his first kill.

"I got all that mob that came our way," he said, "seven of 'em. Yours makes eight. There's Ben after some still, and there's Tommy Prince back at the bamboos firing at something. Firing this way, too, damn him! Look at Ben!"

Far away on the plain, like puppets in the distance, went the swiftly gliding figures of man and horse. In front of them dimly-seen objects tore through the grass; every now and again out went an arm, there was a spurt of smoke, and another buffalo fell. The blacks and the Chinaman were away behind, gathered in a cluster, skinning the first beast killed, while the pack-horses cropped the grass and bit at the flies. Considine was nowhere to be seen.

"Let's go back and see what Tommy is up to," said the shooter. "He's a hard case, is Tommy. If there's any trouble about he'll get into it, or get somebody else into it. He'll wing one of us in a minute, the way he's blazing. What's he firing at?"

Suddenly the festive Tommy was seen to dash hurriedly out of the patch of bamboo, with the old original buffalo cow so close to his horse's tail that, if the horse stumbled, the cow had him at her mercy.

"She'll have 'im!" yelled the shooter. "Good cow! Can't she steam? Come on, and let's see the fun!"

For a while it looked any odds on the cow; then she slackened pace, wheeled round, and bolted back to the bamboos. They found Tommy very excited. He had used about eighteen cartridges, and had nothing to show for it.

"That's the most underhand cow ever I seen!" said Tommy. "She runs into them there bamboos and pretends she's going to run right clean through to Queensland, and when I go in after her, she wheels round and hunts me for my life. Near had me twice, she did. Every time I fire the old carbine, it jams, and I have to get the rod to it. Gimme your rifle, Walter, and I'll go in and finish her."

"She must have a lead mine in her already," said the shooter. "Mind she don't ketch you, Tommy."

Tommy went in, but couldn't find a sign of the cow. While they were talking she had slipped along the belt of bamboos, and was then, no doubt, waiting for a chance to rush somebody. As no one cared to chance riding on to her in that jungle, she escaped with the honours of war. The other shooter came up, having shot nine, and reported that Considine had had a fall; his horse, not being used to the country, had plunged up to his shoulders in a concealed buffalo-wallow, and turned right over on him. Luckily, the buffalo he was after was well ahead, and did not turn to charge him, but he was very much shaken; when he came up, however, he insisted on going on. They set to work to find the rest of the dead buffaloes—no easy matter in that long grass—and all hands commenced skinning. This job kept them till noonday, when they camped under some trees for their midday meal, hobbling the horses. Then they rested for an hour or two, packed the hides on the pack-horses (and heavily loaded they were, each hide weighing about a hundredweight), and went back to the hunt, scanning the plain carefully.

They were all riding together through a belt of timber, the blacks and the Chinaman being well up with the pack-horses, when suddenly the blacks burst out with great excitement.

"Buff'lo! Buff'lo!"

Sure enough, a huge blue bull—a regular old patriarch, that had evidently been hunted out of a herd, and was camping by himself in the timber—made a rush out of some thick trees, and set off towards a dense jungle, that could be seen half a mile or so away. Hugh and Considine were nearest him, each with his rifle ready, and started after him together, full gallop through the timber. The old man was evidently anxious to make up for his morning's failure, and to take Hugh down a peg, for he set a fearful pace through the trees, grazing one and gliding under the boughs of another as only a trained bush-rider can. Hugh, coming from the mountains, was no duffer in timbered country either, and the two of them went at a merry pace for a while. The bull was puzzled by having two pursuers, and often in swerving from one or the other would hit a tree with his huge horns, and fairly bounce off it. He never attempted to turn, but kept straight on, and they drew on to him in silence, almost side by side, riding jealously for the first shot. Considine was on the wrong side, and had to use the carbine on the near side of his horse; but he was undeniably a good rider, and laughed grimly as he got first alongside, and, leaning over, prepared to fire. Then a strange thing happened. Before he could fire, the buffalo bull tripped on a stump and fell on his knees, causing Considine's horse to shoot almost past him. As the bull rose again, he sprang savagely sideways, bringing his huge head up from beneath, and fairly impaled the horse on his horn. It gave a terrible scream, and reared over.

The old man never lost his nerve. Almost as he fell he fired down into the buffalo's shoulder, but the bullet had no effect. Man and horse were fetched smashing to the ground, the man pinned under the horse's body. The bull hesitated a second before hurling himself upon the two; and in that second Hugh jumped from his horse, ran up, stood over the fallen man, holding out the rifle like a pistol with the muzzle an inch off the bull's head, and fired. A buffalo's skull is an inch and a half thick, solid bone, as hard as granite; but a Martini carbine, sighted for a thousand yards, will pierce it like paper at short range. The smoke had not cleared away when the huge beast fell to the ground within two feet of his intended victims. Hugh pulled Considine from under the horse. The unfortunate beast struggled to his feet, with blood gushing from a terrible wound in the belly, ran fifty yards, and fell dead.

The old man looked round him in silence. "Serve me damn well right," he said at last. "I ought to have got the other side of the buffalo!"

Not another word did he say, as he transferred his saddle to one of the blacks' horses. But in the camp, that night, the old man came over to Hugh holding a paper in his hand.

"I've got something for you," he said. "Here's the certificate of my weddin' with Peggy Donohoe. The parson gev us each one. That ought to do you, oughtn't it? I'll come down with you, as soon as you like, and give all the evidence you want. I'll chance how I get on with Peg. I'll divorce her, or poison her, or get shut of her somehow. But after what you done to-day I'm on Grant's side, I am."

And off he stalked to bed, while Hugh talked long with Tommy Prince and the buffalo-shooters of the best way to get down to the wire and send the news of his success. He went to bed the happiest man south of the line; and next day, saying good-bye to his hospitable friends, he started off with Considine and Tommy on the road to the telegraph, and thence to civilisation.

CHAPTER XXVII
THE REAL CERTIFICATE

As the day of the great case approached Blake got more and more restless and irritable. He had heard of Hugh's going away to look for a witness; but Peggy and Red Mick, in their ignorance, had thought it best to keep all knowledge of the Considine flaw from their lawyer—a mistake that wiser people than they sometimes make. Blake suspected nothing. He had more than once seen Mary Grant and Ellen Harriott in Tarrong, but he was again an outcast, relegated to the society of such as Isaacstein.

Well, he would see it out, and would yet make these people glad to crawl to him. Ellen Harriott he never spoke to. However the case went and whoever won, she could be of no use to him, so he decided to include her among his enemies; and though she went deathly white when she saw him she made no sign of recognition. There was one thing, however, which he had to do before taking the case into Court, and that was to secure a fair share of the spoil for himself. He had no intention of slaving at the case, perhaps for years, for what he would get as costs. So, a week or two before the case was due to come on, he sent for Peggy and Red Mick.

It was a hot summer day when Peggy came in. Out of doors there was a blinding glare, and the heat had drawn the scent out of the unseasoned pine with which Tarrong was mostly built, till the air was filled with a sort of incense. Peggy came in hot and short-tempered. The strain was beginning to tell on her nerves, and, from a remark or two she let fall, Blake saw that she might be inclined to give trouble if not promptly brought into subjection.

"I've sent for you," he said.

"Yis, and the fust thing—"

He interrupted her sharply.

"The first thing is, how much am I going to get out of this case if I win it? That is the first thing. You don't suppose I am going to spend time and money and fight this case through all the Courts in the land, and get nothing out of it, do you? How much am I to get? We'll settle that before we go any further."

"Well, I'll ask Mick."

"You'll ask nobody. Mick isn't Grant's widow, and you are of age, goodness knows. How much?"

"How much d'ye want?"

"I want one-third of what you get. That'll leave you nearly a million of money. There will be well over a million to divide. There will be a big lawsuit, and lots of appeals, and if I am to see it through it will cost a great lot of money; so if I win I mean to make it pay me. That's my figure. One-third. Take it or leave it."

Peggy wriggled about, but knew that she would have to give in. It was a reasonable proposal, as things stood; but she did not like the way in which she had been bullied. She looked at Blake queerly.

"If we have to give ye a third, ye may as well know all about it. Ye'll be a partner like."

Blake stared at her. He could not guess what she was driving at. Peggy slowly drew out of a handbag a faded piece of paper and handed it to him without a word. It was the original marriage certificate, the same that Ellen Harriott had seen at Red Mick's. He unfolded it and spread it out on the table.

"What's this?"

"Read it."

"I certify that I, Thomas Nettleship," he mumbled through the formula, then, sharply "What's this name doing here? Who is Patrick Henry Keogh? Is there such a person?"

"Yis," said Peggy, boiling up. "A long slab-sided useless feller. He's gone to live wid the blacks. He'll never come back no more. Most like he's dead by this time, speared or the like of that!"

For a few seconds Blake, the cool, audacious gambler, was dazed, in spite of his natural self-confidence. He saw how he had been duped. Peggy had married this other man, whoever he was, and had used the facts of the real marriage to give her the details for her imaginary one, while in copying the certificate she had, with considerable foresight, filled in Grant's name instead of that of Keogh.

All Blake's castles in the air, his schemes for revenge, his hopes of wealth, had vanished at one fell swoop. "Patrick Henry Keogh" seemed to grin up at him out of the paper. His case had crumbled about his ears; his defeat would be known all over the district, and nothing could much longer stave off the inevitable exposure of his misappropriations. But he was a fighter all over, and he still saw a chance to pull things through.

He wasted no words on Peggy. "Go and get Mick to come here," he said, and Mick, still somewhat lopsided about the face from his accident, was soon in the room.

"Mick," said Blake, "your sister has told me something very important that ought to have been told me before. It's no good crying over spilt milk. There's still a chance. If Peggy and Martin tell the same story they told me at first, they will win the case. This Keogh must be dead, or too frightened to show up. If you stick to your story you will win. It's a million of money. Will you chance it?"

"What about the sertiffykit?" said Mick.

"Leave that to me," said Blake. "I'll see to that. I suppose no one knows the rights of this but you and Peggy!"

"Never a soul."

"Well, it's a million of money. Will you chance it?"

Mick and his sister rose. "We'll go on wid the case," said Mick. "But supposin' Keogh turns up—"

"You've got to take chances in this life," said Blake, "if you're after a million that doesn't belong to you. Will you chance it? Share and share alike?"

"A million," said Mick. "Of course we'll go on wid the case. I daresay William Grant took the name of Keogh that day he was married," and with this ingenious suggestion Mick took his sister home, leaving Blake alone in the office.

After his clients were gone Blake looked at the certificate for a long time, asking himself, "Shall I take the risk or not?" He was about to do a criminal act, and though it was not his first, he flinched every time he crossed the border-line. He lifted his hand, and hesitated; then he remembered his dismissal from Kuryong, and caught sight of a dunning letter lying on his table. That decided him. The risk was worth taking. The danger was great, but the stake was worth it. He took an eraser, made a few swift light strokes on the paper over the almost illegible writing, and "Patrick Henry Keogh" disappeared; on the space that it had occupied he wrote "William Grant," in faint strokes of a pencil. He had crossed the border-line of crime once more.

CHAPTER XXVIII
A LEGAL BATTLE

And now, after hauling the reader pretty well all over Australia—from mountain-station to out-back holding, from cattle-camp to buffalo run—we must ask him to take a seat in the Supreme Court at Sydney, to hear the trial of the "great Grant Will Case."

Gavan Blake had made no effort towards compromise. He knew the risk he was running, but he had determined to see it through. The love, the ambition, the hope that had once possessed him had turned to a grim desperate hatred, and he would risk everything rather than withdraw the case. He kept Red Mick and Peggy up to the mark with assurances that she was certain to win. Neither he nor they knew that Considine had been found. Even the most respectable solicitors sometimes display acuteness, and the old man's return had been kept secret by Pinnock, so that public opinion anticipated Peggy's victory.

At last came the day of trial. Every seat in the Court was filled, and a mass of the unwashed hung over the gallery rail, gazing at the show provided for their entertainment. Mary Grant and Mrs. Gordon went into Court at the suggestion of their leading Counsel, Bouncer, Q.C., who was nothing if not theatrical. He wanted them there to see the overthrow of the enemy, and to lend point to his invective against the intruders who were trying to take away their birthright. A small army of Doyles and Donohoes, who had come down for the case, were hanging about dressed in outlandish garments, trying to look as if they would not tell a lie for untold gold. The managing clerks were in and out like little dogs at a fair, hunting up witnesses, scanning the jury list, arranging papers for production, and keeping a wary eye on the enemy. Punctually as the clock struck ten, the Judge strutted into Court with as much pomp as a man-of-war sailing into a small port; depositing himself on the Bench, he glared round for a few seconds, and said to the associate, "Call the first case," in a matter-of-fact tone, just as if he did not know what the first case was going to be. A little rustle went round the Court as people settled themselves down for the battle.

The case for Peggy was set forth by the great Jewish barrister, Manasseh, Q.C. He was famous for his skill in enlisting the sympathies of the jury from the outset. He drew a moving picture of the sorrows of Peggy, disowned by her husband's relatives and the case proceeded so far that he had put the marriage certificate in evidence when Blake, who had been away for a few minutes rushed into Court and touched Manasseh on the shoulder, bringing him to an abrupt stop.

Manasseh asked the Judge to excuse him for a moment while he conferred with his juniors and Blake. After a short but excited conference he rose again and—but first we must hear what had happened outside.

While all concerned were in Court listening to Manasseh, Considine had been smuggled into the witnesses' room and, being bored and worried, had strayed into the verandah of the Court buildings. He had been hauled into consultations with barristers, and examined and badgered and worried to death. The hard Sydney pavements had made his feet sore. The city ways were not his ways, and the mere mental effort of catching trains and omnibuses, and keeping appointments, and having fixed meal-times, was inexpressibly wearing to a man who had never been tied to time in his life.

And what a dismal prospect he had before him! To go over to England and take up a position for which he was wholly unfitted, without a friend who would understand his ideas, and in whom he could confide. Then his thoughts turned to Peggy—Peggy, square-built, determined, masterful, capable; just the very person to grapple with difficulties; a woman whose nerve a regiment of duchesses would fail to shake. He thought of her many abilities, and admitted to himself that after all was said and done, if he had only been able to gratify her wishes (and they did not seem so extravagant now) she would have been a perfect helpmate for him. His mind went back to the weird honeymoon at Pike's pub., to the little earthen-floored dining-room, with walls of sacking and a slab table, over which Peggy presided with such force of character. He thought of the two bushmen whom Peggy had nursed through the fever with rough tenderness; and then, turning suddenly, he found Peggy standing at his elbow.

For a second neither spoke. Then Considine said, with an air of forced jauntiness, "Well, Peggy, you won't be comin' to England with me, then?"

"Haven't been asked," said Peggy.

"I heard you was goin' to settle at Kiley's Crossin', lending money to the cockatoos."

Peggy looked at him with a meaning glance.

"Ye should know me better nor that, Paddy," she said.

This cleared the way tremendously. The gaunt bushman hitched himself a little nearer, and spoke in an insinuating way. "I'm pretty tired of this case meself, I dunno how you feel about it."

"Tired!" said Peggy. "I'm wore out. Fair wore out," and she heaved a sigh like an elephant.

That sigh did for old Considine. Hurriedly he unburdened his mind.

"Well, look'ee here, Peggy—I've got whips of stuff now, and I've got to go to England for it. You come along o' me again, and we'll knock all this business on the head. Let the Gordons alone—they're decent young fellows, the both of 'em—and come along o' me to England. That young English feller reckons we'd be as good as the Prince of Wales, very near. Will you come, Peggy?"

It is the characteristic of great minds to think quickly, and act promptly. Peggy did both.

"Mick!" she said, calling to her brother in a sharp, authoritative voice: "Mick! I've been talking to Paddy here, and we've reckoned we've had enough of this fooling, and we're off to England. You go in and tell old Fuzzy-Head" (she meant the Judge) "that I'm tired of this case, and I ain't goin' on wid it. Come on, Paddy, will we go and get some tea?"

"Yes, and there's some tremenjus fine opals in a shop down this way I'll buy you!" said Considine, as they started to walk away from the Court.

At that moment Blake came out of Court, saw them, and stepped in front of Peggy.

"Who is this man?" he said.

Peggy had never quite forgiven his domineering at Tarrong, and turned on him with a snap.

"This is my 'usband," she said, "Mr. Patrick Henery Considine. Him whose name is put down as Keogh on the marriage stiffykit I give you."

Then Blake knew that he had played and lost—lost hopelessly, irretrievably. But there was yet something to do to secure his own safety. He rushed back into Court, and whispered a few words to Manasseh; and Manasseh, after the short conference we mentioned some pages back, rose and informed the Court that his client withdrew her claim. Now, while Blake was out of Court, Mr. Bouncer, Mary's counsel, had got from the Judge's Associate the certificate that had been put in evidence. Ellen Harriott, sitting with Mary and Mrs. Gordon behind him, gave a little cry of surprise when she saw the paper. She touched Mr. Bouncer on the shoulder, and for a few seconds they held an excited dialogue in whispers.

So Mr. Bouncer rose as Manasseh sat down, with a smile of satisfaction on his face.

"I must object to any withdrawal, your Honor," he said. "My client's vast interests are still liable to be assailed by any claimant. I wish your Honor to insist that the case be heard. A claim has been made here of a most dastardly nature, and I submit that your Honor will not allow the claimants to withdraw without some investigation. I will ask your Honor to put Gavan Blake in the box."

Mr. Manasseh objected. He said that there was no longer any case before the Court; and Gavan Blake, white to the lips, waited for the Judge's decision. As he waited, he looked round and caught the eye of Ellen Harriott. Cool, untroubled, the heavy-lidded eyes met his, and he saw no hope there. She had neither forgiven nor forgotten.

Now, it so happened that the Judge felt rather baulked at the sudden collapse of the big case, in which he had intended to play a star part.

"Why do you want to put plaintiff's attorney in the box, Mr. Bouncer?" he said.

"I want to examine him as to how and when the name of William Grant got on that certificate. I have evidence to prove that the name on it, only a few months ago, was that of Patrick Keogh."

"Ha, hum!" said the little Judge. "I don't see—eh—um—that I can decide anything—ah—whatever. Case is withdrawn. Ha, hum. But in the interests of justice, and seeing—seeing, I say," he went on, warming to his work as the question laid itself open before him, "that there is serious suspicion of fraud and forgery, it would be wrong on my part to allow the case to close without some investigation in the interests of justice. As to Mr. Manasseh's objection, that the Court is *functus officio* so far as this case is concerned, I uphold that contention; but, in exercise of the power that the Court holds over its officers, I consider that I have the power—and that I should exercise the power—of putting the solicitor in the box to explain how this document came into its present state. Let Mr. Blake go into the box."

But while the little Judge was delivering his well-rounded sentences, Blake had slipped out of Court and made off to his lodgings. He had failed in everything. He might perhaps keep out of gaol; but the blow to his reputation was fatal. He had played for a big stake and lost, and he saw before him only drudgery and lifelong shame.

He had reached his lodgings, half-turned at the door, and saw behind him the Court tipstaff, who had been sent after him.

"The Judge wants you back at the Court, Mr. Blake," said the tipstaff.

"All right. Wait till I run up to my room for some papers. I'll be down in a minute," and he ran upstairs.

The tipstaff waited cheerfully enough, until he heard the crack of a revolver-shot echo through the passages of the big boarding-house. Then he rushed upstairs—to find that Gavan Blake had gone before another Court than the one that was waiting for him so anxiously.

CHAPTER XXIX
RACES AND A WIN

After the great case was over life at Kuryong went on its old round. Mary Grant, now undisputed owner, took up the reins of government, and Hugh was kept there always on one pretext or another.

Considine and his wife stayed a while in the district before starting for England, and were on the best of terms with the folk at the homestead, Peggy's daring attempt to seize the estate having been forgiven for her husband's sake.

Mary seemed to take a delicious pleasure in making Hugh come to her for orders and consultations. She signed without question anything that Charlie put before her, but Hugh was constantly called in to explain all sorts of things. The position was difficult in the extreme, although Peggy tried to give Hugh good advice.

"Sure, the girl's fond of you, Mr. Hugh!" she said, "Why don't you ask her to marry you? See what a good thing it'd be? She's only waitin' to be asked."

"I'll manage my own affairs, thank you," said Hugh. "It isn't likely I'm going to ask her now, when I haven't got a penny." He was as miserable as a man could well be, and was on the point of leaving the station and going back to the buffalo camp in search of solitude, when an unexpected incident suddenly brought matters to a climax. A year had slipped by since William Grant's death, and the glorious Spring came round again; the river was bank-high with the melting of the mountain-snows, the English fruit-trees were all blossoming, and the willows a-bud. One day the mailman left a large handbill, anouncing the Spring race-meeting at Kiley's, a festival sacred, as a rule, to the Doyles and the Donohoes, at which no outsider had any earthly chance of winning a race.

In William Grant's time the handbill would have soon reached the fireplace; he did not countenance running station horses at the local meetings. Under the new owner things were different. Charlie Gordon was spoiling for a chance to run Revoke, a back-block purchase, against the locals, and suggested it in an off-hand sort of way while reading the circular. Hugh opposed the notion altogether. His opposition apparently made Miss Grant determined to go on with the scheme, and she gave Charlie *carte blanche* in the matter.

When race-day arrived, there was quite a merry party at the homestead. Carew was making himself very attentive to Ellen Harriott, Mary was flirting very openly with Charlie Gordon, to Hugh's intense misery; and it was whispered about the station that the younger brother would be deposed in favour of the elder.

Hugh did not want to go to the races, but Mary asked him so directly that he had no option.

It was a typical Australian Spring day. The sky was blue, the air was fresh, the breeze made great, long, rippling waves in the grass, and every soul in the place—Mary in particular—seemed determined to enjoy it to the utmost.

Revoke, the station champion, came in first in his race, and was promptly disqualified for short weight, but Mary didn't care.

"What is the use of worrying over it?" she said. "It doesn't really matter."

"I have been done," said the bushman. "Red Mick lent me the leadcloth, and helped me saddle up, and I believe he took some lead out while we were saddling. It never dropped out. That I'm sure of."

"Oh, never mind, Mr. Gordon! Forget it! There's your brother, Hugh, thinks we ought not to have come, and now you are turning sulky. Why do all you Australian people amuse yourselves so sadly?"

"I don't know what you mean by sadly," said Charlie, huffed. "I think you ladies had better go home soon. Things are likely to be a bit lively later on. They have got a door off its hinges and laid on the ground, and a fiddler playing jigs, and the men and women are dancing each other down; it won't be long till there'll be a fight, and somebody will get stretched out."

Sure enough, they could see an excited crowd of people gathered round a fiddler, who was playing away for dear life, and the yells and whoops told them that partisanship was running high. All the young "bloods" of the ranges were there in their very best finery—cabbage-tree hat (well-tilted back, and secured by a string under the nose), gaudy cotton shirt, and tweed trousers of loud pattern, secured round the waist by flaring red or green sashes. In this garb such as fancied themselves as dancers were taking their turns on the door. They began by ambling with a sort of strutting walk once or twice round the circumscribed platform; then, with head well back and eyes closed, dashed into the steps of the dance, each introducing varied steps and innovations of his own, which, if intricate and neatly executed, were greeted with great applause. So it happened that after Jerry the Swell, the recognised champion of the Doyles, had gone off with an extremely self-satisfied air, some adherents of young Red Mick, the opposition champion, took occasion to criticise Jerry's performance. "Darnce!" they said. "Jerry the Swell, darnce! Why, we've got an old poley cow would darnce him blind! Haven't we, Mick?"

"Yairs," said young Mick, with withering emphasis. "Darnce! He can't darnce. I'll run, darnce, jump, or fight any man in the district for two quid."

Before the challenge could be accepted there was an unexpected interruption. Hugh had put the big trotting mare in the light trap for Miss Harriott and Mary to drive home. "Gentle Annie" was used to racing, and Hugh warned the girls to be careful in starting her, as she would probably be excited by the crowd, and then turned back to pack up the racing gear and start the four-in-hand with the children. As they were putting the racing saddle, bridles, and other gear into the vehicle, Charlie, who had been fuming ever since his defeat, caught sight of the missing lead-bag. He picked it up without a word, and with a fierce gleam in his eye, started over to the group of dancers, followed hurriedly by Carew. Just as young Mick was repeating his challenge to run, jump, dance, or fight anybody in the district, Gordon threw the lead-bag, weighing about six pounds, full in Red Mick's face.

"There's your lead, you thief!" he said. "Dance on that!"

Red Mick staggered back a pace or two, picked up an empty bottle from the ground, and made a dash at Gordon. The latter let out a vicious drive with his left that caught Mick under the ear and sent him down like a bullock. In a second the whole crowd surged together in one confused *melée*, everybody hitting at everybody amid a Babel of shouts and curses. The combat swayed out on to the race-course, where half a dozen men fell over the ropes and pulled as many more down with them, and those that were down fought on the ground, while the others walked on them and fought over their heads. Carew, who was quite in his element, hit every head he saw, and knocked his knuckles to pieces on Black Andy Kelly's teeth. The fight he put up, and the terrific force of his hitting, are traditions among the mountain men to this day. Charlie Gordon was simply mad with the lust of fighting, and was locked in a death-grip with Red Mick; they swayed and struggled on the ground, while the crowd punched at them indiscriminately. In the middle of all this business, the two ladies and Alick, the eldest of the children, had started Gentle Annie for home, straight down the centre of the course. The big mare, hearing the yelling, and recognising that she was once more on a race-track, suddenly caught hold of the bit, and came sweeping up the straight full-stretch, her great legs flying to and fro like pistons. Alick, who was sitting bodkin between the ladies, simply remarked, "Let her head go!" as she went thundering into the crowd, hurling Doyles and Donohoes into the air, trampling Kellys under foot—and so out the other side, and away at a 2.30 gait for at least half a mile before the terrified girls could pull her up, and come back to see what damage had been done.

That ended the fight. The course was covered with wounded and disabled men. Some had been struck by the mare's hoofs; others had been run over by the wheels; and a great demand for whisky set in, under cover of which Gordon and Carew retired to the four-in-hand.

No one was seriously hurt, except "Omadhaun" Doyle, who had been struck on the head by the big mare's hoof. He lay very still, breathing stertorously, and Jerry the Swell took the trouble to come over to the four-in-hand, and inform them that he thought "Omadhaun" had got percussion of the brain, and that things looked very "omnibus" for him. However, as soon as he could swallow whisky he was pronounced out of danger, and the Kuryong party was allowed to depart in peace for home, glad enough to get away. But the two girls were afraid to drive the big mare, as she was thoroughly roused after her dash in among the Doyles and Donohoes, and was inclined to show a lot of temper. A hurried consultation was held, with the result that Ellen Harriott and Alick were received into the four-in-hand, while Hugh was entrusted with the task of driving his employer home in the sulky.

Now, a sulky is a vehicle built to accommodate two people only, and those two people have to sit fairly close together. For a few miles they spun along in silence, Hugh being well occupied with steadying the mare. From time to time he looked out of the corner of his eye at his companion; she looked steadily, almost stolidly, in front of her. Then she began to tap on the floor of the sulky with her foot. At last she turned on him.

"Well, we didn't win," she said. "I suppose you are glad."

"Why should I be glad, Miss Grant?"

"Oh! you said we oughn't to go and race among those people. And you were right. It served them just right that the mare ran over them. I hope that none of them are going to die."

"They wouldn't be much missed," said Hugh wearily. "They have started stealing the sheep again."

"Can't you catch them?" she said, with pretended asperity. "If you went out and hid in a fallen tree, don't you think you could catch them?"

Hugh looked at her to see if she were in earnest, but she looked straight in front again and said nothing, still keeping up the slight tapping of her foot. He flushed a little, and spoke very quietly.

"I think I'll have to resign from your employment, Miss Grant. I don't care about stopping any longer; and I will go out back and take up one of those twenty-thousand-acre leases in Queensland. You might put Poss or Binjie on in my place. They would be glad of a billet, and they might catch Red Mick for you."

"Do you really want to go?" she said, looking straight at him for the first time. "Why do you want to go?"

"Why?" he burst out. "Because I can't bear being with you and near you all day long, when I care for you, and you don't care for me. I can't eat, or sleep, or rest here now, and it's time I was away. You might give me a good character as a station-manager," he went on grimly, "even though I can't catch Red Mick for you. I'll get you to make out my cheque, and then I'll be off up North."

She was looking down now. The sun had gone, and the stars were peeping out, and in the dusk he could catch no glimpse of her face. There was silence for a few moments, then he went on talking, half to himself. "It's best for me, anyhow. It's time I made a start for myself. I couldn't stay on here as manager all my life."

Then she spoke, very low and quietly.

"You wouldn't care to stay on—for anything else, then?"

"How do you mean for anything else, Miss Grant? You don't want me for anything except as manager, do you?"

"Well," she said, "you haven't asked me yet whether I do or not!"